Bullying in the Churches

Bullying
in the
Churches

Stephen Finlan

CASCADE *Books* · Eugene, Oregon

BULLYING IN THE CHURCHES

Copyright © 2015 Stephen Finlan. All rights reserved. Except for brief
quotations in critical publications or reviews, no part of this book may
be reproduced in any manner without prior written permission from the
publisher. Write: Permissions. Wipf and Stock Publishers, 199 W. 8th Ave.,
Suite 3, Eugene, OR 97401.

Cascade Books
An Imprint of Wipf and Stock Publishers
199 W. 8th Ave., Suite 3
Eugene, OR 97401

www.wipfandstock.com

ISBN 13: 978-1-62564-722-1

Cataloguing-in-Publication Data

Finlan, Stephen.

    Bullying in the churches / Stephen Finlan.

    X + Y p. ; 23 cm. Includes bibliographical references and indexes.

    ISBN 13: 978-1-62564-722-1

    1. Bullying in churches—Prevention. 2. Conflict management. I. Title.

BF637 .B85 F55 2015

Manufactured in the U.S.A.   05/26/2015

Contents

Introduction

MANY OF US WERE inspired to preach the gospel, and we committed our lives to a church, only to find out, upon seeing the inner workings of our church, that it was not based on a healthy foundation. How is it that the place where we go for healing and inspiration has become a center of bullying and power grabbing, at many levels within the organization? How has the place that is supposed to show Jesus' spirit in action become the home of dishonesty?

Do any of these stories resonate with your experience?

As part of her seminary education, a student is given a supervised ministry assignment in a large inner-city church. She arrives with anticipation and hope. Time passes. The senior pastor does not set up the supervisory committee that is supposed to meet with the student until near the end of the first semester, and the committee's report is not finished by the seminary's due date. When the student asks the senior pastor about it, she is told "You are not so important; you are just a small piece within this church. The paperwork will get done." The report in the second semester is also not turned in by the deadline, and when the student asks the pastor about it, she is yelled at.

A student finishes his master of divinity degree and gets his first assignment as an assistant pastor. One of his duties is to lead a Bible study. He asks the participants of his Bible study to write some responses to a passage from Isaiah, but the activity is interrupted by the senior pastor, who stops people from writing and announces, "They don't want to write about that; just ask them general questions." When the assistant pastor goes to the pastor a few days later to ask why that was done, the senior pastor says, "These people don't do biblical analysis. You don't know what they can do. *I* know." The pastor then asks to see the assistant pastor's teaching plan for the Bible study, and tosses out most of what the assistant had planned, insisting that this congregation does not want to analyze what Isaiah said.

A pastor organizes a choir among poor and homeless clients of the church, and they perform a skit with music on Sunday. At the coffee hour following the service, some congregation members make sarcastic comments, even though some of the poor singers are within earshot; one refers sarcastically to the "tuneless choir"; another responds, "or the *toothless* choir," and there is some chuckling.

What is wrong with this picture? Why is there bullying and cruelty in the churches? Aren't we supposed to "bear one another's burdens" (Gal 6:2), to be "building up the neighbor" (Rom 15:2), and to love our neighbors as ourselves (Matt 19:19)?[1] Yet, it is likely that everyone who has spent any time in the churches knows that bullying (usually emotional and personal, rather than physical) is quite common in the churches. Wherever there are different levels of power and prestige in a relationship, or where there is competition for power and prestige, there may be bullying—not just on the school yard. It happens in our houses of worship as well.

I intend in this book to look at many aspects of bullying. I will not name names, nor indicate particular denominations, but will draw upon recent experiences people have had in many different Protestant denominations. There are additional and different dynamics in Catholic churches, but someone else needs to write *that* book.

1. The NRSV is the default translation used.

Abbreviations

Col	Colossians
1 Cor	First Corinthians
2 Cor	Second Corinthians
Eph	Ephesians
ESV	English Standard Version
Gal	Galatians
KJV	King James Version
Matt	Matthew
NASB	New American Standard Bible
NCV	New Century Version
NEB	New English Bible
NRSV	New Revised Standard Version
Phil	Philippians
Phlm	Philemon
Prov	Proverbs
Ps	Psalm
Pss	Psalms
Rom	Romans
RSV	Revised Standard Version
SBL	Society of Biblical Literature
SBLDS	Society of Biblical Literature Dissertation Series
Wis	Wisdom of Solomon

1 - The Problem and the Response

Biblical Antecedents

OF COURSE, BULLYING HAS been around from the beginning. We see it in many Bible stories. Sometimes the reasons for the bullying are given. Joseph's brothers hated him because he was their father's favorite, and when he told them his dream, "they hated him even more" (Gen 37:3–5). They thought him arrogant, "this dreamer." Conspiring to kill him, "they took him and threw him into a pit," but then settled on merely selling him into slavery (Gen 37:18–19, 24–27). The story of Joseph's eventual forgiveness of his brothers (Gen 45:4–24) is one of the most remarkable stories of reconciliation in world literature.

Pharaoh's oppressing of the Israelites was a kind of bullying, even though it happened at the level of the state and was enacted upon a whole community. He "oppress[ed] them with forced labor . . . and made their lives bitter with hard service" (Exod 1:11, 14). He felt threatened by their physical vigor and fertility. Nor are the later Jewish kings free of political bullying. King Jehoiakim had Uriah—who "prophesied against this city"—murdered (Jer 26:20–23).

We know that Jesus was bullied, as well. The Roman cohort stripped Jesus, crowned him with thorns, mocked him by saying "Hail! King of the Jews!," spat on him, and struck him (Matt 27:28–30). But the religious leaders' attacks on Jesus were just as bad. Besides instigating the case against Jesus in the first place, the "chief priests" and scribes mocked Jesus on the cross, saying "he saved others; he cannot save himself"; they joined the Romans and the thieves in taunting him (Matt 27:41–44; Mark 15:31–32). Whence comes this arrogance and cruelty of secular and religious authorities?

Such cruelty is all too common. The Epistle to the Hebrews speaks of the "enlightened . . . being publicly exposed to abuse and persecution . . . suffered mocking and flogging" (Heb 10:32–33; 11:36). Paul expects apostles to be treated like the dregs of society, made "a spectacle to the world . . . beaten . . . like the rubbish of the world, the dregs of all things" (1 Cor 4:9, 11, 13). Will new ideas always meet such vicious opposition?

And does this abuse have to happen within the church, as well? No. We need to watch out for it, in order to prevent it. We need a behavioral ethic that works proactively against abusive behavior. We need to take the love mandate as seriously as Paul did: "Through love become slaves to one another" (Gal 5:13). This is an intense commitment, but a necessary one. Without love, we are nothing more than a social club. But if we start practicing the difficult but transformative ethics of Jesus, the church becomes a force for the only kind of social change that is deep and long-lasting—change that is based upon transformed *individuals*.

Instead, we see behaviors that look like the "same old same old," and make us wonder if the church has made any difference in people's lives. Love is the litmus test that shows whether we are serious about our faith: "We know that we have passed from death to life because we love one another. Whoever does not love abides in death" (1 John 3:14). Do we really hold ourselves up to this standard? Or do we have selfish cliques, corrupt leaders, or power bases organized to prevent certain kinds of change? Can our self-image as a loving people stand up to thoughtful examination? How honest are we with ourselves?

The Worldly Church

We should not really be shocked or surprised to encounter sinful behavior in church. The churches reflect the world, and this world is made up of flawed people who create "enmities, strife, jealousy, anger, quarrels . . . factions, envy," and more (Gal 5:20–21). The way of the world infects the church, eroding the foundations that Jesus established. People who are tenderhearted but unskilled at political infighting sometimes get swept out of the church. This turns out to be nothing new. The Apostle Paul, with some sarcasm, warns against ill will in the church: "If you bite and devour one another, take care that you are not consumed by one another" (Gal 5:15).

Even people who have good intentions for the welfare of the church can become very competitive and jealous when they think someone is intruding on their particular mission. Longtime church volunteers tend to develop a strong sense of ownership of the church or a particular aspect of it in which they have long been involved. Experienced volunteers can become very prickly about intrusions on "their" territory. Even if the conflict that ensues stops short of "biting and devouring," it can easily lead to "anger, quarrels, dissensions, factions" (Gal 5:20).

Despite our religious rhetoric, we are sensitive human beings who can get our feelings hurt if we feel we are being disrespected. Also, we are often *unconscious* human beings who are unaware of the extent to which our narcissistic selfishness is infecting our service activities. A pastor cannot always discern beforehand just how sensitive a particular church volunteer may be, or how likely they may be to take offense at any perceived intrusion on "their" territory. Managing these relationships can be very tricky, and may require extraordinary patience on the part of the pastor.

We need to lubricate our relationships with plenty of love, so that when disagreements happen, they happen within a relationship where love already exists, and the disagreement can be discussed calmly. A healthy church will have debates and disputes, but will keep them within the enfolding presence of love and respect. Almost any problem can be solved if people remember to act respectfully toward others. But narcissism and manipulation can undermine the functionality of a church, leading to territorialism, factionalism, and various kinds of attacks. The manipulator may be skilled at *cloaking* his or her real motives, and the attempt to reach mutual understanding could be met with contempt. The territorialist has an exaggerated sense of self-importance, and a sense of entitlement and grandiosity. Of course, pastors can fall prey to these behaviors, as well.

Healthy respect and self-respect are legitimate needs. Genuine mutual respect is a two-way street that requires generous and forgiving attitudes on both sides of the relationship. If one side harbors a grudge or clings to territory, there will not be much progress in resolving conflict. And if the church is not a place where ethics are practiced, why would people want to join?

There are certain kinds of church members who look for ways to exercise power and pronounce judgment within the church. Thomas Bandy calls them "controllers." They "gravitate to positions of power particularly on official boards, finance committees, trustees, property committees, personnel committees. . . They roam through the body of Christ judging, micromanaging, blocking initiative, and generally damaging the cells of the body."[1]

A blog by James McGrath touches on the subject of longtime church volunteers who bully and push people around. The blogger bemoans that some churches are "held hostage by volunteers. . . . Who is going to rebuke someone who is always fixing things around the church?"[2] McGrath hopes that churches can become places where "bullying instincts" can be overcome. This needs more intensive study, I think, since the tendencies of self-assertion and protective controlling or "caring" are widespread, and most churches have not made a priority of examining the psychology of bullying or the ethics of power.

Another writer sarcastically suggests that "being a church bully is good business these days. . . . Bullies are often supported

1. Bandy, *Road Runner*, 89–90.

2. McGrath, "Bread and Bullying"; "Exploring Our Matrix" blog entry for December 16, 2013.

in a small group that likes to keep up on the latest church gossip.
. . . As a bully, you can find allies who are ready to support you,
who will offer behind-the-scenes support to your behind-the-
scenes bullying. . . . People will worry that challenging bullies is
unkind or unchristian."[3] Parker says anyone in any position can
be a bully—the hard part is that "Standing up means risking being
unpopular."[4]

Kenneth Haugk wrote an influential book some years ago
that addressed the problem of toxic individuals and cliques in
the church, whom he calls "antagonists." He makes it clear that he
does not use "antagonist" to refer to "people on different sides of
an argument" or to the "Honorable Opposition"; he is referring to
people who "go out of their way to make insatiable demands, usually attacking the person or performance of others. These attacks
are selfish in nature, tearing down rather than building up."[5]

Dennis Maynard makes similar observations after interview-
ing forty pastors who had been hurt by antagonists in their congregations (and using twenty-five of these cases for his book): "We can
no longer afford the luxury of denying that there are dysfunctional
personalities in congregations that want to hurt clergy."[6]

The problem is not just with laypeople, of course. It also exists
with clergy, especially those who aspire to rise within the regional
organization. Eager to ingratiate himself with his district superintendent, a member of a district committee may go along with
anything the DS does, even "piling on" when the DS has decided
to target someone. Piling onto a chosen scapegoat is a common
technique for winning approval from higher-ups. This shows that
the ancient patronage system has not disappeared; it's still *who* you
know, not *what* you know.

---

3. Parker, "Twelve Reasons Why It Is Good to Be a Church Bully" on the
site "The Millennial Pastor."

4. Ibid. The article is followed by a helpful conversation among many
participants.

5. Haugk, *Antagonists in the Church*, 25–26.

6. Maynard, *When Sheep Attack!*, third page of the Introduction, no page
number given. Maynard's website is Episkopols.com.

Self-serving careerism is probably as common in the churches as it is in other fields of employment, although it is somewhat disguised in the attempt to deny its contradiction of biblical values. Hypocrisy thrives in the gap between our declared values and our real motivations. Values (the ones really *practiced*) create a certain atmosphere, encouraging certain behaviors. If we value control above all else, we will be competitive and suspicious. We create an atmosphere for conflict. Bullying thrives in such an atmosphere.

Maynard's study is quite sobering. He affirms Haugk's observation that there are certain antagonists who intend to do harm to a pastor. Maynard makes it clear that he is not talking about those who offer constructive criticism, even *sharp* criticism occasionally, but about those who set out "to hurt, humiliate, destroy and remove the senior pastor."[7] What was most shocking to me in his book was the high degree of complicity of the bishops in the mistreatment of clergy. Of the twenty-five cases that form the basis of Maynard's study, when accusations against the pastor came in, "only a couple of the bishops in our survey even bothered to check with the clergy and the healthy parish leadership to determine if the accusations of the antagonists were true."[8] Most of the bishops in the cases he examined either remained passive or actively joined with the antagonists; even worse, the leader among the antagonists was often a retired or active clergyperson, or even a retired bishop.[9] It is not just in Maynard's denomination that this goes on.

Most churches have an ethical procedure for handling grievances, and they need to use it. In most churches, however, there is not much in the way of established procedure for handling misbehavior by laity. There should also be some thoughtful teaching, preaching, and even training in the prevention of slander and bullying. Forgiveness does not mean that we protect or give free reign to the thing (bullying, in this case) that is being forgiven. There is amazing forgiveness in Jesus' kingdom, but that does not mean

7. Maynard, *When Sheep Attack!*, 13.
8. Ibid., 114.
9. Ibid., 103–5, 110, 113.

that there are no consequences, no adjudication, no education, no therapy.

What about the psychology of antagonists? They seem to be people who hold on to resentment, who feel deeply wronged in their lives, but are only dimly aware of how long they have felt this way, and are even less aware of how their vengeful feelings against people in the present are fueled by how they were treated in the past. The antagonist has never taken a long hard long at himself and his psychopathology.

People who are unable to recognize their own spiritual poverty and are unwilling to exercise any reflective self-criticism are displaying the classic signs of narcissistic personality disorder, on which there will be a section at the end of this chapter, but first there is more to say about group process.

An Atmosphere for Bullying . . . or Respect

If there is immaturity and selfishness within a group, and no process for prayerfully listening to differing points of view in the congregation under wise pastoral leadership, then blaming, bullying, and territorialism will manifest themselves. The gospel solution involves teaching and learning some interpersonal skills that can limit the destructive effects of bullying, and possibly even get the bully to examine himself. Some gospel-informed techniques include learning to discern and appreciate the good motives of others, consciously showing mutual respect, seeking understanding, and cultivating a generous and forgiving attitude.

Pastors, of course, need to be wise as well as harmless (Matt 10:16), shrewd as well as kind. The principle of learning to see the good motives of others may include learning to bracket out the bad motives that the pastor thinks s/he sees, at least until such time as an evil pattern of behavior is confirmed beyond a doubt.

At the risk of oversimplifying, I would graph these problems and solutions like this:

Problem	Solution: The Right Attitude	Practical Application
Factionalism	Mutual appreciation of others' motives	Respect for differences
Territorialism	Mutual respect	Sharing, conferring
Blaming	Understanding, forgiving	Open discussion with attentive listening
Bullying	Empathy	Anti-bullying discourse and publicity

Why does "love" not appear in the solution or application columns? Because *all* of these solutions and applications involve love. Some involve practicing forbearance and forgiveness in the present ("Bear with one another and, if anyone has a complaint against another, forgive each other," Col 3:13). Some involve taking the long view: having faith that God is working within the other person ("the one who began a good work among you will bring it to completion by the day of Jesus Christ. . . . It is God who is at work in you," Phil 1:6; 2:13).

But this is spiritual hard work, and many people strongly resist it. It is much easier to divide the world into allies and enemies, to dish out all blame to the latter, and to not do the hard work of self-critique. When enough people in a group decide to avoid inner work as well as interpersonal work, then conflicts will only get worse. When the love process breaks down, when feelings become inflamed, positions entrenched, and indignation stoked, respect is forgotten, and the group starts to look for a "fall guy" to blame. Sometimes it is the spiritual leader who becomes the target of mean-spirited political maneuvering.

There can also be pressures that come from outside the religious group. Political-religious pressures from outside Jesus' group, and at least one disgruntled voice among his disciples, led to a conspiracy against Jesus. The religious authorities felt threatened by his liberating message and his authoritative presence. Jesus knew that he would "undergo great suffering, and be rejected by the elders" (Mark 8:31), as had happened to many of the prophets before him (Luke 11:49).

In fact, every honest critic, every reformer, every nonconformist undergoes rejection, usually starting within the immediate family. Jesus was even said to be "out of his mind" either by townsfolk or by his family (Mark 3:21). And he commented more than once on the sad fact that "Prophets are not without honor except in their own country and in their own house" (Matt 13:57; and see Mark 6:4; John 4:44). To be a brave and original thinker is not an easy path to tread. Such a person must be ready to be treated "without honor." It seems to be a law, a tedious, painful law of life, that those who manifest excellence and originality are usually resisted, resented, even punished "in their own country."

Jesus was surprised that his apostles did not recognize this pattern. Did they not realize "about the Son of Man, that he is to go through many sufferings and be treated with contempt? But I tell you that Elijah has come, and they did to him whatever they pleased" (Mark 9:12–13). This last comment refers to the cruel treatment of John, thrown in a dungeon and then beheaded at the whim of an aristocrat's daughter. Herod Antipas, who authorized the killing of John, was a bully from a long line of bullies. Herod represents the way of the world, the way of people when their selfishness is not restrained, when their minds are not enlightened by the gospel. It is not a Jewish characteristic or a Gentile trait; it is a common *human* feature. The unspiritualized human being, grasping after power and security, is a bully.

What is more surprising to many of us is to find deliberate cruelty going on in our churches, to find political maneuvering and backbiting in the board of trustees, the finance committee, and the choir. When did church become all about power, control of turf, "my way or the highway"? When did Christians become so worldly? Actually, this is nothing new; we see selfish competition among the apostles, and factionalism in the early church. Slander and backbiting can become contagious in a church. Cruelty and bullying seem to be the way of the world, and the churches are all too worldly.

One Gospel story begins with the apostles arguing "as to which one of them was the greatest" (Luke 9:46). Could they have been any more selfish? This is where Jesus shocks them by using a child to show them that "the least among all of you is the greatest" (9:48). The apostles will get into the same dispute again later, and he will have to tell them that a *real* leader is a servant (Luke 22:24–27; Matt 20:25–28). Of course, many church bullies are also volunteers who "serve" the church, but their service is poisoned by aggressive behaviors, the psychological roots of which are unconscious. Religious people can practice a moralistic and judgmental kind of bullying, commonly recognized as a "holier-than-thou" attitude.

Jesus as Defender of the Vulnerable

Jesus defended many individuals against bullying, and took steps to restore their self-respect. As he was walking through Jericho, he encountered a blind man begging. The blind man, finding out that Jesus was walking through the town, shouted to him, "Jesus, Son of David, have mercy on me!" (Luke 18:38). The crowd that was with Jesus "sternly ordered him to be quiet," but he shouted all the more. Jesus had the man brought near and simply asked him, "What do you want me to do for you?" Healing him, as the man requested, Jesus finished by saying: "your faith has saved you" (Luke 18:42). Jesus builds up the self-respect and praises the faith of this man whom others were trying to silence. I cannot imagine this man being silent ever again! He would have been a beacon of praise and gratitude from that time on.

Perhaps even more embarrassing (in that day and age) than a blind beggar was the woman with an issue of blood, who approached him as he was on his way to heal someone else. Here is another person shunned by her society, "suffering" (Mark 5:25), and bent over by shame. Yet she musters the courage to secretly approach Jesus, to touch his garment, and gets healing even from that timid step of faith. Jesus calls her forward and "she came trembling" (Luke 8:47), but he gently encourages her, saying "take heart, daughter; your faith has made you well" (Matt 9:22). Would anyone dare to shun her again? Would Levites and priests cross the street when they saw her coming? Or would they shun her for a different reason, because of the story she now undoubtedly had to tell?

Another important instance of Jesus stopping an act of bullying was when a woman was being criticized for anointing his feet. Jesus leaped to her defense: "Let her alone; why do you trouble her? She has performed a good service for me" (Mark 14:6). Notice that his main concern is that people "let her alone"—stop criticizing her. All too often we focus on the Christology in this passage, but what about the simple kindness, the compassion of Jesus? That is where he begins: "let her alone." He stands up for her in the face of a contemptuous crowd of people (including his own followers) who were considered socially superior to the woman. His defense of her is a defense of human spirituality, in opposition to labels of class, gender, and reputation. *We* should begin there, too, affirming respect for every child of God.

When the people of Jericho grumbled against Zacchaeus the tax collector, with whom Jesus said he would be staying, he defended the man, building up his self-esteem with the remark "Today salvation has come to this house, because he too is a son of Abraham" (Luke 19:9). He could not have said anything more confidence-building than this! The man is a son of Abraham, the friend of God and father of the faithful. In *that* society, one gets to take on some of the prestige of one's ancestors, so Zacchaeus, *too*, is faithful, and a friend of God. What a different message than the sneering attitude of the townspeople toward Zacchaeus!

In these four examples, we see Jesus uplifting people who had been marginalized because of deformity, impurity status, gender, and profession. But the most celebrated instance of Jesus' defense of marginalized people happened when the apostles rebuked children for coming up to him. Jesus not only defended them ("let the little children come to me"), but "he was indignant" with the apostles (Mark 10:14), and he held children up to be emulated. Jesus says "the greatest in the kingdom" is the one who "becomes humble like this child" (Matt 18:4), something completely counterintuitive to the way we *still* think. He is highlighting the child's trustingness: adults must be *receptive*, must "receive the kingdom of God as a little child" (Mark 10:15; Luke 18:17), and that means they must "change" (Matt 18:3). The receptivity of children is the standard by which one gains admission to the kingdom.

No other sage or prophet, no founder of a religion is so well-known for showing a high regard for children. There will be more to say about this in the section on Jesus' critique of the patronage system. Here we must point out that Jesus also stood up for adults who were unjustly criticized. When his apostles were accused of breaking the Sabbath by gleaning, he defended them with two biblical stories, capping it off by saying, "If you had known what this means, 'I desire mercy and not sacrifice,' you would not have condemned the guiltless" (Matt 12:1–7). The criticism arose out of a fixation with ritual rules; the critics did not know the value of "mercy" (or "compassion," NASB). God desires compassion more than any ritual observance, and the obsession with ritual correctness can lead to bullying—religious bullying. Fixation upon purity rules is devoid of love. Today there are many Christians (on both the Left and the Right) who have a kind of purity system which they use to judge and bully those who do not rank highly on their purity scale.

Jesus offered many lessons that militate against bullying, such as parables in which he exalts people from despised groups: a good-hearted Samaritan (Luke 10:25–37), a self-effacing tax collector (Luke 18:13–14), a merchant who wants pearls (Matt 13:45–46). He works against the common bias against Samaritans, who had a variant version of Israelite law and cult. He questions the popular resentment of tax collectors, even having a tax collector as one of his apostles (Matt 9:9). He even undermines the smug contempt for merchants, building a spiritual teaching on the image of the merchant's love for fine jewelry. There is something useful even in human connoisseurship. He repeatedly mocks the "holier-than-thou" attitude of those who looked down on merchants, tax collectors, women, and Samaritans.

Further, he undermines the contempt for foreigners several times, commending a Roman centurion and a Syro-Canaanite woman, and he even travels to Gentile territories (Mark 5:1; 7:24; Matt 15:21) and interacts with Gentiles. He honors a centurion because the man recognizes order in the universe ("I say to one, 'Go,' and he goes, and to another, 'Come,' and he comes," Matt 8:9), and knows that Jesus has a position at the top of the spiritual order ("only speak the word, and my servant will be healed," 8:8). The Syro-Canaanite woman is honored for her faith, her persistence, and perhaps even her sense of humor, though it may be that the evangelists do not recognize her humor. (I see humor in Mark 7:28/Matt 15:27, but Jesus' reaction in the following verses in those gospels does not indicate any recognition of that humor).

Jesus showed so much love for ordinary people, for needy people, for children, even for Gentiles, that any description of his personality must emphasize this feature. When faced with cruelty, he could comment on it with objectivity, without wrath. After being struck by a temple guard, Jesus said "If I have spoken wrongly, testify to the wrong. But if I have spoken rightly, why do you strike me?" (John 18:23). If the guard had any conscience he would have felt shame after this. Jesus calmly appealed to the guard's sense of justice, trying to reason with the bully. Experience shows that this usually does not work; once people start acting violently, they become moral cowards, and their conscience is stifled. We do not know what the result was in this case. There was at least one person with whom this worked: the centurion at the cross, who, after Jesus' death, said "Truly this man was a son of God."[10]

The most amazing statement of forgiveness was when Jesus forgave his killers from the cross (Luke 23:34). Again, his

10. The noun *huios*, "son," without any article, should be translated "*a* son." The NRSV gives this as a marginal translation in Mark 15:39 and Matthew 27:54.

considerate approach gave people a chance to exercise their conscience, if they hadn't suffocated it completely. What we always see is that, although he was mistreated, he did not revile; "he did not return abuse" (1 Pet 2:23).

Jesus responded to the guard's bullying by making a calm and truthful statement about improper behavior, but it requires a sensitive observer for this to take effect. The truth will be preserved if there is any sensitive observer (like the centurion) to appreciate it. This may be one of the meanings of "Let anyone with ears listen!" (Matt 11:15; 13:9; Mark 4:23). Truth is handed on by anyone who *hears* it. Jesus presents it as a gift; not saying that we *must* hear him, but that anyone who *can* hear him shall receive what he is giving. Truth is a gift that blesses all who receive it, not a hammer that pounds people into obedience.

Jesus responded to his killers with the merciful statement that they really did not know what they were doing. Jesus lets the success of his message be entirely dependent upon the chance that a sincere listener is present, and on the listener's quality of reception. In this way, Jesus has faith in *us*, in our ability to "hear." In this way God waits for us to be ready. Do we have ears to hear? Will we respond, or will we seek to break God's heart? Many people truly have a streak of vindictiveness and hostility toward God, and they take revenge on God by being cruel to people.

Jesus understands this, and many other psychological complexities. He has remarkable insight into human character; his forgiveness is not naïve, but happens with eyes wide open. He calmly observes how self-deceived his enemies can be, and warns his disciples, "an hour is coming when those who kill you will think that by doing so they are offering worship to God" (John 16:2). Rationalization springs eternal in the human breast. Even people who are conspiring to commit murder can convince themselves they are doing right. Jesus knows about the tendency to rationalize, to twist the truth for selfish reasons, and he trains his apostles to recognize it in those who mistreat them.

We live in an age where the insights of psychology have deepened and broadened our understanding of human misbehavior, but we need to go further. Christians need to become more psychologically aware, so that we are not helpless when sin happens. Wisdom "will save you from the way of evil, from those who speak perversely" (Prov 2:12). Jesus modeled calmness, compassion, and trust in people's receptivity to the truth, but also a firm stance against cruelty and hypocrisy.

The Narcissist

It is time to look at a recognized psychological malady: narcissistic personality disorder. Not every bully is a narcissist, but many of them are, and these are the people least responsive to kind and compassionate overtures of any kind. The reader can decide if these features sound familiar.

First it is important to state that there is a natural "residue of childish narcissism, i.e., the child's natural self-love," and that a "severe impoverishment" in the child getting its narcissistic needs met will tend to make more difficult "the later absorption of this narcissism into more mature self esteem."[11] So *some* residue of narcissism is considered normal. We are not talking about this normal phenomenon when we speak of narcissistic personality disorder (NPD). The standard definition of NPD, from the *DSM-IV*, is "A pervasive pattern of grandiosity (in fantasy or behavior), need for admiration, and lack of empathy."[12] People with this disorder are obsessed with power and self-importance; they cannot tolerate criticism and they lack empathy. While the person with mature self esteem will moderate his own claims in consideration of the views of others, the narcissist will devalue and disdain others, and "respond with despair and rage when their pressing narcissistic needs/demands were not responded to."[13] They frequently express contempt while secretly envying others. A person with narcissistic personality disorder will be

11. Erikson, *Identity*, 70–71.

12. American Psychiatric Association, *Diagnostic and Statistical Manual of Mental Disorders IV*, from http://www.halcyon.com/jmashmun/npd/dsm-iv.html.

13. Randall, *Pastor and Parish*, 13–14.

"extremely sensitive to failures, disappointments, and slights. . . . To real or imagined slights, he responds with shamefaced withdrawal and depression, or with 'narcissistic rage.'"[14] Unlike psychotics, who suffer from personality disintegration and delusional states, narcissists are relatively stable and socially functional.[15] They can "play the game," and hold on to leadership positions for years, but their lack of empathy and moral principle injects poison into human systems.

We have to face the fact that techniques for handling normal conflicts simply will not work with narcissists. Chilling though it may be, there are people in the church who are "evil, who target moral leaders (usually pastors) for destruction."[16] A narcissist who is making a grab for power can lie without a twinge of conscience, and there is no way to have a constructive conversion with someone who lies. Negotiation is a useful technique for handling most conflicts, but it will not work when the complaint is coming from a narcissist, who does "not have a normal rational process."[17]

A wholly different tack is taken by Randall and the field known as self psychology, founded by Heinz Kohut. This school of thought insists that narcissistic needs are normal, even in adulthood, but some people are better able to cope with the frustration of these needs, and some people lack good self-cohesion. Self psychology does not say that everyone is the same, but it does say that everyone has the same basic underlying narcissistic needs. I think this theory has much to offer, but its rhetoric is complicated and technical, and it may have limited usefulness in practical settings. However, its insights are important enough to receive some attention here.

Randall describes the three basic narcissistic needs that everyone has, although every individual will have a *primary* need among the three: the need to be mirrored and affirmed, the need for an ideal leader to look up to and from whom to borrow self-respect, and the need to have like-minded fellows. Randall writes: "Pastors

14. Ibid., 34, 46.

15. Kohut, *Analysis of the Self*, 4; Randall, *Pastor and Parish*, 78.

16. Rediger, *Clergy Killers*, 123.

17. Ibid., 85.

and parishes long to feel whole and secure. Their selves reach out for responses that confirm that they are admired, immersed in the specialness of significant figures, and surrounded by like-spirited others"; both pastors and parishes may have "pressing narcissistic needs."[18] Kohut discovered the second of these needs when he noticed that many of his patients would start to show signs of recovery only if they could make a connection with Kohut and experience him as an ideal parental figure. But, "Inevitably, the narcissistically disturbed individual experienced Kohut as flawed and failing. When this happened . . . a wide spectrum of rageful reactions also poured out at the one who had dared to be so insensitive."[19]

Randall looks at individuals and groups in relation to these needs. Every congregation has a sort of "personality" or culture deriving from its unique constellation of narcissistic needs and "and the quality of its self-cohesion."[20] Churches, like individual pastors, have primary narcissistic needs and have varying levels of self-cohesion. A pastor or a congregation with weak self-cohesion will experience chaos, despair, and fragmentation if its narcissistic needs are not met.

Everyone has a natural need "for mirroring acclaim,"[21] for affirmation. The second category, idealizing needs, is where parishioners "whose self-cohesion is weak" manifest a need to "find their selves uplifted, supported, and spiritually nurtured by being in resonating contact with the revered pastor."[22] I tend to have contempt for this need, thinking that people ought to be adults and to stand on their own two feet, which shows that this is not *my* primary need. Self psychology has opened my eyes to the view that this is a normal and expected need for many people, and that we have to allow for it. The third level, where one seeks cohorts or fellows who have similar understandings to oneself, seems perfectly

---

18. Randall, *Pastor and Parish*, 118.

19. Ibid., 40.

20. Ibid., 117.

21. Ibid., 105.

22. Ibid., 108.

normal to me, which probably reveals that this one is my own primary narcissistic need.

Randall talks about narcissistic injuries or "narcissistic depletion and rage," when there is a mismatch between the congregation's longings and the pastor's leadership, or even where there is an "unempathic disregard for the pastor's personhood."[23] If the self of pastor or parish is weak, and they are not shored up with loving relationships, then "depressive withdrawal and lifelessness" may follow, for either pastor or parish.[24] I know of a person who withdrew from a church for over a year, complaining of too many names on the mailing list and other obscure matters, but never telling the pastor what her real complaint was. She maintained a relationship with a previous pastor and waged an angry campaign against the current pastor from a distance, writing a negative letter to the district superintendent and broadcasting a passive-aggressive public letter full of vague complaints, never mentioning the pastor but praising a ministry in the church run by someone else. Somewhere underneath all this bluster and hostility was undoubtedly some legitimate need, but it was never expressed.

The problem is not narcissistic needs, since we all have them. The problem is "archaic needs" (stemming from childhood) that are not expressed in an adult and rational manner. A wise "pastor attempts to help them gradually transform these immature structures into internalized, empowering, creative-productive ambitions and goals."[25] I read this to mean that the keys are maturity and transformation, with ethics being implied. To make self psychology useful for me, I need to heighten the key themes of ethics, maturity, and transformation, and occasionally use more colloquial terms such as "control freak" or "a complete transformation of attitude." I think most readers have some idea of what those terms mean. I can understand that a clinical psychologist would want to be more precise, to identify which of the three narcissistic needs is being frustrated for a particular individual, but I think

23. Ibid., 127.

24. Ibid., 122.

25. Ibid., 156.

most of us care less about that than about whether the person's behavior is considerate and respectful of others. Is the person mature or not? Is the person experiencing spiritual transformation or not? These are the key questions for most of us.

Self psychology may help us to recognize that all people have selfish needs, and thus get us to recognize the gray area in human affairs, but sometimes we need to sharply distinguish between black and white. Sometimes we simply need to know whether or not it is safe to talk to a person, whether that person will become enraged by any attempt to have a dialogue.

Rediger's much less clinical approach may be helpful here. Rediger speaks of a sequence of "agendas" or psychological needs. At the bottom are a person's survival needs, where *feelings* are dominant; above that are identity needs, where *thinking* is dominant; the highest level is relationship needs, where thinking and feeling can be integrated.[26] There are negative and positive emotions on each of the three levels. When one's survival feels threatened, one feels fear. When one's identity is threatened (often the case when attacks take place in church), one feels anger.[27] When relationships fail, one feels sadness. To some degree, Rediger's three levels can be made to correspond to the three different narcissistic needs of self psychology: the survival level pairing with the need to be praised, the identity level corresponding with the need to have an idealized caretaker, and the relationship level to the need for fellow thinkers. But again, it seems clear that, for practical purposes, we can focus primarily on the need for maturity, ethics, and transformation.

There can be no transformation for an unreflective person, someone who sees no need to change. The narcissist refuses to accept that there is any problem with his/her behavior or thinking. If members of a congregation are growing spiritually, the stagnant narcissist will stick out like a sore thumb. Only in a spiritually crippled congregation can a narcissist fit in nicely and not be recognized by others as someone who is not experiencing growth and transformation.

26. Rediger, *Clergy Killers*, 113.
27. Ibid., 115, 117.

2 - The Jesus Response

JESUS WAS VERY MUCH aware of bullying behavior, and he stressed, especially to his apostles, a new and higher law for responding to mistreatment: "Love your enemies, do good to those who hate you, bless those who curse you, pray for those who abuse you" (Luke 6:27–28). This was an unexpected response, and one whose practice demands enormous strength of character. And Jesus practiced what he preached: "When he was abused, he did not return abuse; when he suffered, he did not threaten" (1 Pet 2:23). We saw this in his calm question to the bullying guard in John 18:23.

How difficult it is to live this way! There are some hard truths about this way of living, but first I should start where Jesus himself started.

The Easy Yoke

Jesus said "my yoke is easy, and my burden is light" (Matt 11:30). There is a theme of joy running throughout Jesus' teachings, even though he anticipated how his life would end, worried about the difficulties that his apostles would face, and mourned for poor, foolish Jerusalem. And yet joy—and the *teaching* about joy—were central for Jesus.

In several parables, the kingdom of heaven is linked with the theme of surprising joy: the joy at finding a lost sheep or a lost coin (Luke 15:6, 9; Matt 18:13). In the parable of the Prodigal Son, the father is overcome with joy at the return of his son; he *runs* out and greets him (almost unheard of, in that very status-conscious culture); he orders a feast, and is ecstatic that "this son of mine was dead and is alive again" (Luke 15:20, 24). The other son is disgruntled; "he became angry and refused to go in"; he condemns his brother, who "has devoured your property with prostitutes" (vv. 28, 30). But the father's final word to the hyper-serious son is "we had to celebrate and rejoice, because this brother of yours was dead and has come to life" (v. 32). There was no choice; we *had* to celebrate! Anything else is inconsistent with *life*. And that is one of the keys to Jesus' life and teaching: his *liveliness*, his unpretentious friendliness, his celebration of love and life. It is really the judgmental son who is the "lost son," dwelling in his self-righteousness, unable to rejoice. He is a moralistic bully, quick to judge (vv. 29–30), and possibly even to slander: it is only from *him* that we hear of the prodigal son consorting with prostitutes; nowhere else in the story is this allegation confirmed. Whether or not his report is accurate, he represents a very common type of bully: the morally proud person who is actually full of bitterness, indulging his resentment by judging others harshly. But really, he is punishing himself, excluding himself from his father's joy. Ironically, the embittered and self-righteous bully has become a very common character in Christian churches.

Jesus' parables contain other warnings against this kind of self-righteous moralism, seen also in the indignant attitude of some laborers in the vineyard (Matt 20:11–12) and in the arrogance of the Pharisee who is glad he is not like a tax collector (Luke 18:11).

But humble and honest gratitude brings a harvest of joy. Jesus' way of living is *full* of joy. His way exudes a life-affirming buoyancy that infects others, penetrating the barriers of pride and self-righteousness. It seems to have worked with most of his apostles; the self-assertive John[1] later became the "apostle of love"; the Jesus-denying Peter became the great preacher and leader of the early church; even Simon "the Zealot" (Luke 6:15; Acts 1:13)

---

1. Luke 9:54; possibly Matt 20:21–22.

became a dedicated preacher to Gentiles.[2] Why could we not experience the same character transformations in our churches, changing self-interest into skill at serving others?

Jesus' infectious love and confidence reached those who most needed to be *seen*, to be appreciated and lifted up: the tax collector Zacchaeus, the lunatic of the Gerasenses, the beggar of Jericho, the woman with an issue of blood, the man with the withered hand, the man who was lowered through a ceiling.[3] He raised the self-esteem of all these people, and their lives were forever changed after they heard him say "he too is a son of Abraham," or "take heart, daughter; your faith has made you well," or "Son, your sins are forgiven."[4] Who could *not* be changed by hearing Jesus say "take heart"? How often the world wants to crush us, and take away our heart—but Jesus empowers people to be courageous, to recover their spiritual center.

The kingdom of heaven is discovered with joy, like finding buried treasure (Matt 13:44), or like the angelic joy over one sinner who repents (Luke 15:7). Unless we have learned this, we are not qualified to start talking about the death of Jesus or his willingness to suffer, because our thinking will be distorted by morbidity and superstition. Only if we understand the joy and triumph of Jesus should we dare to speak of his suffering. Only if we know of the *reality* of spiritual triumph can we safely philosophize about the evil in the world. "I have overcome the world" (John 16:33 RSV). "I watched Satan fall" (Luke 10:18). Every day we see the tedious persistence of selfishness in human character, but the gospel tells us that evil will not triumph in the end. The even more persistent love of Jesus will eventually win over the human race. It is fashionable to have a bleak outlook on humanity, but do we remember this promise?—"I came not to judge the world, but to save the

2. Ancient sources give varied reports, but several have Simon spreading the gospel in Egypt and Libya, and giving his life for the gospel (McBirnie, *Search for the Twelve Apostles*, 207–8).

3. Luke 19:1–10; Mark 10:46–52; 5:1–20; Matt 9:20–22; 12:10–13; Mark 2:3–12.

4. Luke 19:9; Matt 9:22; Mark 2:5.

world" (John 12:47). At the very least, this means that "people will come from east and west, from north and south, and will eat in the kingdom of God" (Luke 13:29). But, more than this, it means that "the kingdom of heaven is like yeast that a woman took and mixed in with three measures of flour until all of it was leavened" (Matt 13:33).

All of the human race will be leavened! Do we believe it? Even his enemies knew that he came "to gather into one the dispersed children of God" (John 11:52). *Eventually*, we are taught, "God will be all in all" (1 Cor 15:28 NEB). The conquering love of Jesus is the antidote to the world's bullying.

This is an essential element of the the "good news" teaching that has been neglected of late, in the wake of so much war, injustice, rapid social change, and loss of faith. But without this foundation in unshakable hope and joy, we do not have the whole gospel. A church without joyous hope has forgotten the gospel.

The Hard Truths

There is a difficult side, a demanding side, a willingness to endure in suffering, that accompanies the way of love, focalized in a saying we quoted at the beginning of the chapter: "Bless those who curse you, pray for those who abuse you" (Luke 6:28).

This is so difficult! It is like experiencing ego death. When we are mistreated, everything within us cries out for self-protection, justice, vindication. But in this sinful world, we will not always get that, so we need to learn to practice self-forgetfulness, with God's help. This involves trusting in a vindication that may not be seen in this lifetime. We are asked to believe in a spiritual world that hasn't arrived yet. Can we do it? Can we live as though in the kingdom of heaven—a kingdom that we do not see, but only glimpse in our imaginations? The life of faith is a courageous and often lonely path. We have to believe in our ideals enough to suffer for them, even to see them scorned by people around us. The walk of faith is not for cowards.

In the way of faith, there is simultaneously a grasping and a letting go. We grasp onto God and onto the principles of faith that we get from the Gospels. We affirm the goodness of God and the certainty of the eventual triumph of truth. But there is at least as much *letting go* as there is *grasping*. This means getting the ego to let go of control, and getting our self-protective side to let go of defensiveness. This letting go is counterintuitive; it feels risky because it *is* risky. There is no guarantee of how the world will treat us.

Nevertheless, we have our assignment: "do not worry . . . have faith . . . pray always" (Matt 6:25, 17:20; Luke 18:1), for is it not true that "the kingdom of God is within[5] you" (Luke 17:21 KJV, NCV)? We must learn *a new way to live*. There seem to be three behaviors in which we have to train ourselves:

—The first is to let go of our desire for control and power in the church, whether we are lay or clergy.

—Harder even than that may be to let go of the desire for affection or esteem; to stop thinking, "Can't I demand a little respect? Aren't I entitled to just a little bit of love?" Instead, can we pray "Jesus, help me to let go of a sense of entitlement, of wanting to fight for what I think I deserve"?

—Finally, we need to let go of the desire for security and survival. "Those who try to make their life secure will lose it, and those who lose their life will keep it" (Luke 17:33). This is one of the paradoxical principles that we need to learn if we are to follow Jesus. And we can only learn it by practicing it, not by analyzing it at great length, forcing it to make sense (because, on a strictly worldly or intellectual level, it will *not* make sense). It is hard to accept that we may not get justice or safety in this lifetime.

Power, affection, and security are not bad things; the problem is in *clinging* to these, or making them our central goals. Doing the will of God and seeking to live the godly way should be our singular goal.

5. "Within" is a more accurate translation of *entos* than is the NRSV's "among," but NRSV does offer "within" in the margin. See Finlan, "Deification in Jesus' Teachings," 22–24.

When Jesus forgave his killers, he was practicing courageous and far-sighted love. It was not mushy or weak-minded. It meant looking ahead to a time when those others might come to a realization, might become aware of their sin, might become sick of themselves. Eventually, if people are honest, they *will* become sick of their unhealthy behaviors. We have to trust that God will work in people's souls, even if we don't see it happening as quickly as we would like, or happening *at all* in some people. We must have faith in the ultimate triumph of truth and goodness, beyond what we can see around us; we must have the undergirding reality of Jesus' joy in order to not be disturbed by the temporary triumph of evil.

There seem to be two ways to live:

Worldly Motivation	Jesus Motivation
Using others for selfish ends	Praying for others
Lording things over others	Serving others
Always striving for status	Experiencing ego death
Striving for vindication	Letting go of the desire to be vindicated
Believing only in the material world	Trusting in the reality of the spiritual world
Seeking to control	Letting go of control
Seeking affection	Letting go of the need to be liked
Needing security	Surrendering to uncertainty
Short-sighted goals	Seeking the eternal good of self and others

Having godly motivation is, of course, a gift of God. The ability to love our enemies is not our own; it is the gift of God. Even when we are hated or targeted, we can trust that *God* knows our heart. It is reassuring to know that we will be judged by a perfect and just judge. It then feels less intolerable when we are misjudged and mistreated here. That does not mean that we should be completely passive and accepting of mistreatment; only that we should not expect to get approval from an unenlightened society.

Once we *know*—and *only* if we know—that the truth will be heard in heaven, can we find it natural and normal to "do good to those who hate you" (Luke 6:27). We need to know that only "justice is immortal" (Wis 1:15 NEB). Only goodness and truth will last forever; only a just report will endure. Only what is right and fair will prevail in the long run. In Jesus' universe, certainty about the triumph of good is the only truly *rational* belief. We know that rain *will* fall on the just and the unjust, but we are children of God (Matt 5:45; Ps 82:6), and we have been gifted with an eternal destiny (John 6:47, 11:26).

Of course, Jesus' saying about loving those who mistreat you is not meant to prevent us from taking care of ourselves in our personal lives. It is not meant to hold us in bad relationships, or keep us trapped in any way. In fact, the teaching of Jesus is the key to becoming free from the mental traps of helplessness, despair, and negativism. The nonviolence of Jesus is spiritually aggressive and creative. It does not mean that we must passively tolerate all injustice. In fact, lovingly "turning the other cheek" is an act that creatively confronts the abuser, asking if he intends to continue acting this way. The action makes a strong statement, even if one is verbally silent. It stands as a kind of loving rebuke. Further, it takes charge of the situation. If there is any ethical sensitivity in the person doing the evil or in the crowd witnessing it, the rebuke will "hit home" with someone. Even the perpetrator may eventually realize he has done wrong.

. . . But maybe he will not! Maybe the perpetrator is not being honest, and such a person cannot really be reached.

Although it seems outrageous, it is a fact that some people who attend churches are not considerate, tolerant, forgiving, or even fair; they are not practicing any of the ethics of Jesus. They do not really know Jesus at all, and have internalized nothing of his teachings. They are in the grip of their narcissistic resentment, and they will engage in destructive behavior. Woe to us when we come into their crosshairs.

The worst narcissistic explosions come from people who refuse to face the fact that their problems stem from their childhood, and have nothing to do with their chosen targets in the present moment. There are some very wounded people out there, but the most destructive ones are those who do not take any responsibility for their own healing, who even refuse to admit that they are sick. Here, again, the gospel has something to say. Jesus said he came for the sick and the sinners, not for those who "have no need of a physician" (Matt 9:12–13). We need to have the humility to *know* we are sick, or to *know* we are sinners. Honesty is the key. Any sickness is all right, as long as you are honest with Jesus, with God. The worst sickness is denial, the cold, icy denial of one's own sickness and sin. Those who suffer from it are the people who really cannot be helped. Scott Peck argues this point. He says that the key that makes someone truly "evil is not the sin but the refusal to acknowledge it . . . characterized by their *absolute* refusal to tolerate the sense of their own sinfulness."[6] They refuse to feel or acknowledge their guilt. Peck had one patient who had some evil attitudes, but he *felt guilty about them, and so was driven to change* and to turn his life around. Truly evil people refuse to feel that guilt. "Because in their hearts they consider themselves above reproach, they must lash out at anyone who does reproach them. They sacrifice others to preserve their self-image of perfection."[7] They are especially fond of scapegoating, which is a form of projection; they "attack others instead of facing their own failures."[8] Scapegoating is a technique

6. Peck, *People of the Lie*, 69, 71.

7. Ibid., 73.

8. Ibid., 74.

for preserving our "own sick selves."[9] Such people do not engage in any self-critique. Though they "lack any motivation to *be* good, they intensely desire to appear good."[10] Dishonesty is at the heart of evil: "We become evil by attempting to hide from ourselves."[11]

Jesus was very much aware of the difference between the honest person who can admit his sin or sickness, and the dishonest one who refuses to admit anything. He sharply distinguished the Pharisee who thanked God he was "not like other people" from the humble tax collector who said "God be merciful to me, a sinner!" (Luke 18:11, 13). We sometimes miss the psychological insights of Jesus because they are expressed in the terms of a pre-psychological age. But a closer look, accompanied by an awareness of ancient rhetoric, can uncover the psychological depths. The statement "I have come to call not the righteous but sinners" (Matt 9:13) is a Semitic exaggeration. It means that the call is only *heard* by those who are honest enough to *admit* that they are sick or sinful. The self-satisfied and the self-righteous will not hear his call, but actually Jesus is calling *everyone*.

By using the language of sickness, not just the language of sin, Jesus showed that he was psychologically ahead of his time. Many people nowadays don't relate to the language of "sin"; in fact, they rightly feel *sinned against* more than they feel they have sinned. Jesus offered the other model for them, the model of being "sick." Everybody (everybody who is being *honest*, that is) can identify with one or the other malady: sickness or sinfulness. It is the people who are not being honest about their own sickness who make the worst bullies.

Several authors caution against trying to use normal conflict-resolution or compassionate listening techniques with bullies, since these methods assume some rationality and sense of justice in both parties to a dispute, but bullies are *not* rational or just, and the attempt may just give the bully more opportunity to mistreat the target. June Hunt makes a sharp distinction between "healthy

9. Ibid., 119.
10. Ibid., 75.
11. Ibid., 76.

common conflicts" that are "often unintentional" and where there is a "desire to solve the problem," and "unhealthy bullying conflicts" which are intentional, at least for the bully, who has "no desire to solve the problem."[12] She warns that traditional conflict resolution can lead to further victimization. Mediation usually involves sharing the blame, which is inappropriate in the case of bullying.[13] This is probably the case where Jesus' warning applies: "Do not give what is holy to dogs; and do not throw your pearls before swine, or they will trample them under foot" (Matt 7:6). We need to recognize when our kindness is being trashed, and we need to present a stern face at that point, as God told Jeremiah: "I will make you to this people a fortified wall of bronze; they will fight against you, but they shall not prevail over you" (Jer 15:20).

Haugk gives many warnings about the "antagonist," who does not have an *honest* complaint or a desire to understand, but who wants only to vilify and destroy. Haugk warns "requesting a meeting with an antagonist is asking for trouble"; it is a "false assumption that reason and logic will help the antagonist see things correctly."[14] The antagonist will give a distorted report of any meeting that one has with him. We cannot be as open and trusting toward someone with ill will as we are toward a person with an honest complaint or disagreement. We need to anticipate and avoid situations where we will be abused, or where our words will later be distorted. Jesus does not want us to be victimized; if we are not received with hospitality, then "shake off the dust from your feet as you leave that house" (Matt 10:14). Jesus wants everybody to be treated with respect and to have self-respect. In order to approach that, we need to become more psychologically wise and discerning. Jesus calls us to practice a new and higher spirituality, but also to become "wise as serpents" (Matt 10:16).

12. Hunt, *Bullying*, 14.

13. Ibid., 15.

14. Haugk, *Antagonists in the Church*, 129, 135–36.

The Effect of the Jesus Ethic

Within the Jesus community, believers are to practice an entirely different ethic than is common in the world: "You know that the rulers of the Gentiles lord it over them. . . . It will not be so among you; but whoever wishes to be great among you must be your servant" (Matt 20:25–26). Kindness, not bossiness, is to be the new mark of leadership. And yet, a pastor needs to be able to speak up when it is necessary, to repudiate evil behavior, to say "this must stop."[15]

The gospel is meant to restore self-respect to those who have been damaged, and to restrain excessive self-regard in those who have too much of it already. We see this in the way Jesus reacted to certain individuals, empowering the weak, saying "take heart" to the downtrodden, affirming the pure of heart, but vigorously attacking hypocrites and bullies in positions of power, those who "lock people out of the kingdom of heaven. For you do not go in yourselves, and when others are going in, you stop them" (Matt 23:13). They were bullying people, trying to prevent them from entering the Jesus fellowship. Jesus tears into these religious bullies. The most severe words he ever utters are directed at certain powerful "hypocrites! For you are like whitewashed tombs, which on the outside look beautiful, but inside they are full of the bones of the dead" (Matt 23:27). These shallow but powerful people have wounded the self-respect of sincere and honest people, and Jesus sets out to protect the latter.

In a Jesus-saturated community, there is a different kind of relating that goes on. If Jesus' spirit is active, then relationships are based on mutual respect and consideration for the other. This requires some social and psychological maturity. People need to be free from the mental traps of narcissism, rage, and despair. You cannot have a healthy and loving marriage without a basis in respect and in psychological and spiritual health. The same is true about ministry: it cannot be healthy without *real* respect (not just an outward show of respect) and psychological health. Trying to

---

15. See Rediger's advocacy of "toughmindedness" (*Clergy Killers*, 173).

build either a marriage or a ministry on a basis of disrespectful attitudes is like trying to build a house on sand; it will collapse. So a community where the ethics of Jesus are really practiced will be one where institutions and associations are built upon healthy relationships.

Safe and nonabusive environments will be the result. We are right to try to make our families, our churches, and our neighborhoods healthy and safe environments where people are not abused. We have a right to take steps to make life safe for ourselves and those around us. Jesus' ethic of respect and self-respect needs to be the basis for personal and social ethics in all Christian groups and support networks. This inevitably has an effect on the broader society.

A crucial part of social peace comes when people are able to recognize the values and higher motives of others, and practice respect and sensitivity. Once this is achieved, a kind of spiritual unity can develop, even between people who have different beliefs, different theologies, as long as they are able to recognize each others' genuine spiritual motivation. People who really practice the Jesus ethic do not make enemies out of other sincere practitioners of that ethic who understand the gospel differently. Spiritual unity takes place at the deeper level of values and motivations, not at the more superficial level of mental beliefs. One of the tests of whether you are really practicing the Jesus ethic is that you are able to experience this spiritual unity with Christians who have completely different styles or theologies than your own. Thus, a growing movement toward Christian unity is one of the by-products of serious Christian ethics. In the presence of churches of other denominations, each church and each Christian has abundant opportunity to try to practice the principle of spiritual unity.

The Inner Experience of the Bullied

Some psalmists capture the feeling of being bullied: "the enemy has pursued me, crushing my life to the ground, making me sit in darkness like those long dead. Therefore my spirit faints within me;

my heart within me is appalled" (Ps 143:3–4). "Shame has covered my face at the words of the taunters and revilers" (Ps 44:15–16). Targets of bullying have often described the feeling of being pursued (bullies are persistent), a feeling of darkness or loneliness, and a feeling of being crushed or shamed. In response, despite the pain, most Christians seek to forgive and find a path to reconciliation with the bully, but this noble effort is usually unavailing.

Forgiveness may force one to really *experience* injustice, since the person(s) we are forgiving may be so full of rage that they are not reachable by rational means. Spiritually, they may not understand what forgiveness *is*, and they may not *want* to understand. We may be dealing with people who do not want to change their ingrained evil habits, since they enjoy the manipulative power that their behavior gives them.

So how does this affect the Christian who is attempting to forgive that person? The forgiver may experience very profound and protracted anguish, knowing that his or her honest offer of reconciliation is being cynically refused, and that the other is perpetuating evil and falsehood. This is when the Christian really has to *practice* faith. It may be that God grows closest to us when we feel most abandoned. "The Lord is near to the broken-hearted, and saves the crushed in spirit" (Ps 34:18). "A broken and contrite heart, O God, you will not despise" (Ps 51:17). "Reproach has broken my heart and I am so sick. I looked for sympathy, but there was none" (Ps 69:20 NASB). One may feel that "there is none," but actually there *is* one: "He heals the broken-hearted, and binds up their wounds" (Ps 147:3). Furthermore, God knows what you are suffering: "You have kept count of my tossings; put my tears in your bottle. Are they not in your record?" (Ps 56:8). The Psalms are good to read during times of suffering, as long as we can remember to shine a gospel light on them, and not get drawn into their frequent cries for violent vindication (although we can certainly *understand* those).

There may be times when public dishonor is the only genuinely honorable experience. If "The Lord is near to the broken-hearted," then perhaps we are fortunate to experience the scorn of the public. What does the public know? The public called for Jesus' execution. The public wanted the "flesh pots" of Egypt rather than the dangers of the wilderness (Exod 16:3). But God was closer to the broken-hearted Moses than to the shifting opinions of the shallow-minded public. We may say "I am an object of scorn to my accusers," but let us also say "Let them curse, but you will bless" (Ps 109:25, 28).

Be ready to be treated unfairly if you point out improper behavior in the churches. Be ready to be the black sheep. Give thanks when you are the black sheep and everyone points the finger at you. Jesus knows what it is like to be labeled and misunderstood by his countrymen, even by his own family. Don't lose faith in that tender connection you have to God through Jesus. Jesus knows what you're going through. He has "been there."

Yet, how counterintuitive is Jesus' advice to love our enemies and forgive those who persecute us! It takes enormous strength to nurture no resentment when one is wronged, not even to look forward to future revenge (to "heap burning coals on their heads," Rom 12:20). Jesus leaves no room for vengeful feelings at all. This requires strong faith in the certainty of the eventual triumph of fairness and love. Our own social successes cease to be very important when we are truly dedicated to a higher cause.

We should not worry about when our vindication will come, but rather worry "when all speak well of you, for that is what their ancestors did to the false prophets" (Luke 6:26). Our goal is to "Be merciful, just as your Father is merciful. Do not judge" (Luke 6:36–37).

This can be very hard to practice, especially when we are attacked by fellow Christians. But we have to face the fact that many people in the churches have serious mental and behavioral problems, and may be unconscious of the extent to which they are projecting their childhood rage onto people in the present. The church is in the *world*, and believers often reflect the ignorance that is so common in the world. We will be better equipped to handle the tribulations of church life if we can deepen our psychological and historical understanding.

3 – Causes of Bullying

SIMPLY PUT, THE MAIN cause of bullying is competition for power and status. Bullying is a way of mercilessly demonstrating one's power over others. Bullying behavior can also be observed within the animal kingdom, especially in herd or pack animals, where animals will pick on the ones below them in the "pecking order."

There is plenty of this in human societies, as well. Competition seems to spring eternal within the human heart, not only for money and social power, but for sexual attractiveness, popularity, and the securing of a mate. While there are no sections following entitled "Competition for Social Status" or "Sexual Competition," others have written entire books on these subjects, and the basic facts of human competition are well known to all of us.

I will, instead, start by considering the presence of a herd mentality in churches, and how this leads to the exclusion and mistreatment of selected targets, a process that can be called "scapegoating." This leads to consideration of an important theory about scapegoating offered by the philosopher René Girard. Any discussion of how groups "gang up" on a victim needs to consider Girard's writings, especially since he shows how religious groups are prone to scapegoating behaviors. And this is true even if one does not accept all his theories.

The section after that will examine the effect of systematic cruel treatment of children, relying mainly on the work of Alice Miller. After that I will look at one of the ancient causes of bullying, the patronage system, which was very important in the ancient Near East in Jesus' time, and which both Jesus and Paul criticized.

All these different approachs to bullying can be useful for us in understanding why and how bullying happens. I hope the reader is not frustrated by the fact that I investigate all these different approaches. I think the most efficient way to understand, anticipate, and handle bullying is to build up a knowledge base (which includes knowledge gained from experience), and then to synthesize insights and wisdom from each of these approaches. Each one of us will come up with a slightly different synthesis, but that is to be expected. First let us look at a common phenomenon in churches.

The Herd Mentality

A group in a church that senses its dwindling power can undergo certain self-protectionist reactions, such as forming a gang or herd mentality, and looking for someone at whom to direct blame. The most convenient scapegoats are usually a new pastor, new church members, older church members who are not part of the gang, and socially marginal recipients of the church's charitable work. Actually, anyone who is not part of the "old gang" in a church can easily become a target.

The old gang may bitterly resent being labeled as such, or being told that it has a herd mentality. That reveals that much of the psychodynamics here are either unconscious or are the result of lazy-mindedness; in either case, the gang does not want to be identified as such. There is a resistance to self-examination.

The backroom maneuvering of gangs and packs is widespread in the churches. Even when members of the old gang are well-educated, they are likely to be blind to the way they treat those who are not a part of their gang. They may be partially (or *willfully*) unaware of their scapegoating behaviors, their habit of ganging up on a chosen outsider. Or they may be well aware of their scapegoating behavior, but find it easy to justify it. These are the Sadducees of the churches, clinging to their territory, seriously devoted to "their" church, and willing to crush any perceived foe. Lacking self-understanding about their territorialism and controlling behavior, they do not critique their own actions. The old gang sticks together, backing each other up, even members who act unethically or emotionally. What one pastor observed about a particular denomination can be found in other denominations, as well: they "have a herd mentality. They don't want to think about things intelligently or individually. If any of them dislikes something you say or do, then they all begin to dislike you."[1] In a herd, resentment is contagious.

One person I spoke to described a member of such a group by saying "She is part of the Hive. It doesn't matter that she has psychological training; when she enters that church, she is part of the Hive and thinks like the rest of the Hive. 'You criticize any one of us, you threaten the Hive.' They do not ask whether a perceived threat is real or not. Just the *perception* of a threat, to *any* member of the Hive, is enough to trigger the protectionist reaction."

The old gang undoubtedly has its legitimate loyalties and values, but it has become increasingly self-interested, intolerant, judgmental, and prone to pick someone to blame and vilify. The real decisions are made in the hallways or parking lots when the chosen scapegoat is not present. Potential dissenters have been shut out before they even know what the issue is. Churches in the grip of an old gang always seem to be baffled when their pastors become discouraged or burnt out.

The old gang may try to hold on to a favorite liturgy or a fading identity, and can easily feel threatened by a new pastor or by new members of the church. When new members are seen as a threat, a church is well on its way to dying, but the old guard will usually not want to admit that they are cold-shouldering the new people.

In any church, the older members need to have good self-critical skills to be able to avoid unconscious behaviors that drive people away. In a healthy church, the old guard are the most gracious and hospitable people in the community, and they are capable

1. A pastor quoted by Killinger, *Outgrowing Church*, 23.

of self-criticism. They have their views, but they remain flexible; *they are still learning* from life. They are responsible without being tyrannical or judgmental. They do not fear honest self-reflection; they have learned how to grow spiritually. Stated otherwise, they have learned to fight the spiritual battle responsibly, to be honest about their own weaknesses, and generous toward the weaknesses of others (and toward the *strengths* of others!).

We all have to fight an inward battle, and it is reflected outwardly:

> The clash between the creative personality of Christ and the religious mummies of His time is an eternal conflict. In each one of us is both the Pharisee and the true Christian personality which attempts to transcend the lifeless conventionality and dead repetition in our religious life. Christ and the Pharisee are at odds with each other in me. . . . The majority of men have not reached [that] level of maturity. . . . They need a well-structured, conventional frame of living in order to protect them against their own anxiety, insecurity, and timidity.[2]

Those who are unaware of the central importance of the inward battle think that outward forms are what matter; they tend to become obsessive opponents of any change in the liturgy. They also resent the freedom and individuality of anyone who is not as attached to conventional forms as they are. The one who is still a Pharisee inwardly will feel threatened by one who is becoming a Christ inwardly.

Others have written about the herd mentality under different names and in different settings. Doris Lessing writes about how the majority will pressure a minority until "the minority will fall into line . . . nearly always. . . . It *is* a group mind, intensely resistant to change, equipped with sacred assumptions."[3] Eric Voegelin writes about a "tribal" mentality in whole populations, leading to collectivist movements like Nazism and Communism, where the citizen is so "deficient in spiritual organization" that he is eager "to

2. Van Kaam, *Religion and Personality*, 92–93.
3. Lessing, "Group Minds," 49–50.

submerge himself in a collective personality. . . . Tribalism is the answer to immaturity because it permits man to remain immature with the sanction of his group."[4]

Oppressive and abusive groups do not arise out of nowhere; they are the kind of associations that spiritually crippled and psychologically immature people are bound to create. The unbridled atrocities of the Nazis and Communists are really just ordinary bullying and gang behaviors taken to the extreme. Insecure and narcissistic people are adept at denying responsibility for wrongdoing. This can happen at the macro level and with extreme violence, or it can occur at the level of the local church and take the form of unfair and hurtful words. Weak-minded people who participate in or support bullying are able to suppress their qualms of conscience by saying that they are just going along with the majority. If the majority does it, it can't be wrong, can it?

Actually, yes. The majority can become petrified and hostile toward any hint of change. There is one major theorist who would say that the majority is almost always wrong, since it keeps the peace only through scapegoating. It is time to look at René Girard's theory.

Girard's Theory of Scapegoating

René Girard spent over thirty years developing a theory about a repeating pattern of violence in societies. He began with a study of human desire, finding it to be highly imitative, or "mimetic." Girard argued that mimetic desire, along with competition for goods and status, leads to outbreaks of violence. He claimed that all societies, in their prehistory, learned to control violence by channeling it onto a victim. He called this pattern of behavior "the single victim mechanism," or scapegoat mechanism.[5] Afflicted with aggressive desire, humanity learned to avoid eruptions of chaotic violence by focusing the violence on a single victim. The

4. Voegelin, *From Enlightenment to Revolution*, 96–97.
5. See Girard, *I See Satan*, 94.

scapegoating action took on a magical aura when people observed that, "after having been released against the victim, the violence necessarily abates."[6] Competitive power brokers sometimes made peace with each other through the shared selection of a victim, and they were impressed by the sudden abatement of tension and rivalry between them.

Girard argues that religion arose as a technique for covering up the facts and "sacralizing" the violence, mystifying and disguising it. He speaks of "mankind's radical incapacity to understand its own violence."[7] He claims that the sacrificial cult arose as a ritualized cover-up of the scapegoating mechanism. "The sacrificial process furnishes an outlet for those violent impulses that cannot be mastered by self-restraint."[8] Sacrifice and mythology function to mystify, to conceal, and lie about the shared violence against scapegoats.[9]

I do not find Girard's arguments about mythology particularly convincing; they claim to apply universally to all religions and mythologies (as though all myths have the same message). I *do* find his observations very penetrating, however, in particular cases, as when he speaks about the Pharisees, Sadducees, and Romans coming together—natural enemies who were able to unite to commit violence against Jesus. And the aftermath looks like something straight out of Girard's mind: "that same day Herod and Pilate became friends with each other; before this they had been enemies" (Luke 23:12).

The gospel, Girard argues, is the exposé and repudiation of the Satanic pattern of scapegoating. God did not cause the killing of Jesus, but exposed and discredited this pattern of lies and violence. "The synoptic Gospels formally repudiate the conception of a vengeful God."[10] Girard later decided that the whole biblical tradition shared this role of exposing the patterns of violence: "The

6. Girard, *Things Hidden*, 99.

7. Ibid., 180.

8. Girard, *Violence and the Sacred*, 18.

9. Girard, *I See Satan*, 2, 72, 78–80.

10. Girard, *Things Hidden*, 182.

demystification of scapegoating is a specifically Christian and Jewish phenomenon," and he cites the Joseph story as showing that "the victims at the center of myths are innocent."[11] Exposure, then, is the key to breaking the scapegoating habit. One could question whether simple exposure of evil is enough to undermine it, or whether religious leaders can continue to commit scapegoating violence even if their violence has been exposed.

I think Girard has had an important insight, and it illuminates the patterns of dishonesty and groupthink that lead religious groups to conspire in bullying, and to lie about it afterward. Jesus warned his disciples, "an hour is coming when those who kill you will think that by doing so they are offering worship to God. And they will do this because they have not known the Father or me" (John 16:2–3). They have not known the nonviolent Father of Jesus. If they had, they would have ceased their own violence.

We have all read about or seen political scapegoating (and we must remember that Girard grew up in Europe in the immediate post-Holocaust period). Sometimes societies avoid facing their own inner conflicts by selecting a social scapegoat and projecting blame. Putin's Russia has now prohibited "gay propaganda," but everybody knows that this is code language for "we think you should feel ashamed of yourself, and not be seen in public." It is government pandering to a common prejudice, and hinting at the acceptability of bullying the gay "propagandist." Putin's Russia is also bullying the Ukraine and tearing off pieces for itself. The world needs to express its disgust with this political bullying. One weakness in Girard's theory is that it does not account for the widespread *disgust* with bullying, and not just in Christian cultures. Mature and morally sensitive people in any culture are revolted by cruelty.

I think Girard's theory is at its weakest when it tries to explain "religion" as such, and when it tries to attribute the same scapegoating mechanism to *all* societies and to *all* mythologies, treating the latter as though it had only one function. Girardian theory is at its best when it comments on actual instances of religiously

11. Girard, "Violence, Difference, Sacrifice," 31.

motivated mob violence, as when the crowd went along with the suggestion that "it is better for you to have one man die for the people" (John 11:50). The aggression and the scapegoating that Caiaphas practiced do look very "Girardian."

Girard's theory is also useful for observing the dynamics of mob psychology: the infectious nature of fear and aggression, the glee in finding a victim to blame, the new alliances that people form while conspiring, and their dishonest rationalization after they have committed the deed. Most of these same dynamics, minus the physical violence, can be seen in the way that antagonists in a church channel their anxiety by selecting a victim, forming new alliances against the target, slandering that person, and then denying afterwards that they were treating the person as a scapegoat. Bullying can indeed be infectious. The more passive-aggressive people will pile on once they see that the aggressive people have selected a target. There is a certain satisfaction in agreeing with the majority. But it is actually the solace of a coward, the satisfaction of the mediocre, the self-inflation of an empty head.

The gospel fights this disease of imitative bullying. Regarding the mistreatment of John the Baptist and of himself, Jesus said "I tell you that Elijah has already come, and they did not recognize him, but they did to him whatever they pleased. So also the Son of Man is about to suffer at their hands" (Matt 17:12). The bully feels elation while in the process of bullying, but he is trapped in a static condition: "Everyone who commits sin is a slave to sin" (John 8:34). Jesus knew that bullying would continue, hence his warning that true disciples must be ready to "take up their cross daily," and maybe even "lose their life" (Luke 9:23–24; see also Matt 16:24–25; Mark 8:34–35). Now, bullying is draining the life out of some churches.

These two sections have looked at bullying arising out of a herd mentality in churches, and arising out of competition and aggression in societies. Bullying could be analyzed from either of these viewpoints. I think it is helpful to have more than one interpretive model. There are other factors to look at, other approaches to bullying. The next one we will discuss here looks at bullying in the home, and its effects later in life.

Psychological Causes

I will look now at a pattern of psychopathology found in the most extreme bullies: dictators and mass murderers. Of course, what these people do goes far beyond what anyone in our churches is doing, but there are some psychological similarities, and this topic shows us how abuse is handed down through generations.

In examining the childhood of the twentieth century's leading dictators, psychologist and author Alice Miller found that *every one of them* was subjected to extreme cruelty in childhood.[12] We owe a great debt of gratitude to Miller, who exposed to view, first to her fellow Germans and then to the world, the terrible effects of the "poisonous pedagogy"[13] of cruelty to children, which made possible and even "normal" the cruelty of the Nazis. Popular in the nineteenth and twentieth centuries in Germany was a style of childrearing known as "Black Pedagogy," in which parents were encouraged to be very severe and distant with their children as a way of "dealing with 'obstinacy,' willfulness, defiance, and the exuberant character of children's emotions."[14] These German books, assuming that children were inherently rebellious, instructed parents to "drive out willfulness from the very beginning by means of scolding and the rod . . . until . . . all willfulness is gone," and the blows "should not be merely playful ones."[15]

Many people are now breaking the pattern of abuse that they suffered in their childhood. But for many people whom Miller studied, the abuse was handed on: "parents will inflict the same punishment or neglect on their children as they experienced

---

12. Miller, *Paths of Life*, 158, 161–63.
13. Miller, *The Untouched Key*, 101; idem, *For Your Own Good*, 3–96.
14. Miller, *For Your Own Good*, 10.
15. Ibid., 11, 15.

themselves in their early lives."[16] She is talking specifically about parents who were unable to critique or question their own cruel treatment, who came to believe that it was a normal and legitimate way to treat children.

Why is it that *some* children who are severely beaten suffer a kind of inward death and later in life become killers or dictators, while others are able to recognize this treatment as wrong, and to refrain from handing it on to others? It is because for the latter, "there had been at least one person who had shown them honesty, affection . . . even though that person had not been able to protect them." If there is one such "helping witness" in their life, then the person may avoid becoming devoid of empathy later on.[17]

But there are some children who suffer irreparable damage from persistent beatings and suppression of the opportunity to express their suffering, who suffer a kind of inner death, and lose the power of empathy. "They learned to deny their feelings as children. . . . Their souls have become rigid. . . . They have also forgotten how to ask questions" (about what was done to them).[18]

Miller wholly opposes violence against children, refuting the excuse "that this treatment is good for children."[19] On the contrary, cruelty does harm, and the harm is worsened by repression: "the greatest cruelty that can be inflicted on children is to refuse to let them express their anger and suffering except at the risk of losing their parents' love and affection. The anger stemming from early childhood is stored up in the unconscious."[20] "It is not the trauma itself that is the source of illness, but the unconscious, repressed, hopeless despair over not being allowed to give expression to what one has suffered."[21]

The great dictators whom Miller studied all suffered this kind of abuse. "As a boy Hitler was tormented, humiliated, and mocked

16. Miller, *Paths of Life*, 156.

17. Ibid., 155.

18. Miller, *The Untouched Key*, 139.

19. Miller, *For Your Own Good*, 16.

20. Ibid., 106.

21. Ibid., 259.

by his father . . . He denied his true feelings toward his father . . . because hating one's father was strictly prohibited."[22] Stalin was beaten almost daily and "remorselessly" by his father, and he "became hardened by his beatings."[23]

The abused boys who grew up to become Hitler and Stalin learned to repress their true feelings, but then were driven by hatred for the rest of their lives. Similar psychological patterns occurred in the people they got to do their dirty work for them: "The suffering caused by the way you were mistreated will remain unconscious and will later prevent you from empathizing with others. This is why battered children grow up to be mothers and fathers who beat their own offspring; from their ranks are recruited the most reliable executioners, concentration-camp supervisors. . . . They beat, mistreat and torture out of an inner compulsion to repeat their own history."[24]

The dictators are extreme cases, but much of their psychopathology is chillingly similar to what we see in any run-of-the-mill violent husband, raging mother, livid trustee, or vengeful church council member. The murderous dictator is simply able to carry out the rage and revenge to greater effect. Bullying on any scale or at any level is unjust.

Miller's insights apply to "ordinary" families too, ones without any serial killers. It takes someone to become *aware* of the pattern of abuse, to rediscover the suppressed feelings of anger, and to express them with compassion and understanding. The person must learn and recognize that what s/he endured was abusive, and must feel the legitimate anger that this renewed memory will evoke. "If their anger is followed by grief over having been a victim, then they can also mourn the fact that their parents were victims too."[25] The parents might possibly be able to recognize the truth in what their adult child is saying, but only if they themselves are able to do

22. Miller, *Paths of Life*, 158.
23. Miller, *The Untouched Key*, 63–64.
24. Miller, *For Your Own Good*, 115–16.
25. Ibid., 273.

the necessary inner transformative work, and to admit that what was done to them in their own childhood was wrong.

It may be that all church bullies suffered some mistreatment or abuse in the home, and that they have not learned to process these experiences in a mature way yet. It certainly seems to be the case that most church bullies are stuck in destructive habits of behavior: slander, lying, backstabbing, negativity, cliquishness, lust for power. These are not behaviors that can be abandoned overnight; it would require considerable therapy, spiritual counseling, and (most of all) a real desire on the part of the bully to change. It is important that the more mature members of the congregation not only learn to recognize these behaviors as wrong, but also to recognize them as signs of mental and spiritual sickness. This will help the congregation to reflect on courses of action that could— and should—be taken to prevent the whole congregation from being victimized by a few bullies.

Now, in addition to the roles of homelife and psychology, there is a historical social pattern that has contributed to bullying, which I would like to examine now.

The Patronage System

I wish to cover an aspect of bullying that is often neglected: the role of patronage in social competition in the societies of Jesus' time. First it is necessary to say a word about the connection between bullying and other aspects of social behavior. Bullying is not a stand-alone subject. It is shaped by customs and value systems. Sometimes bullying is an attempt to enforce certain cultural values and behaviors. David deSilva writes, "All groups are using the application of honor and disgrace to enforce the values of their particular culture . . . to nurture adherence to group values"; nonconformists will tend to "feel the weight of society's shaming techniques, the insults and abuse calculated to bring them, as deviants, back in line."[26] This kind of enforcement still exists; all of us have

26. deSilva, *Letter to the Hebrews*, 62–63, including note 2.

probably met those defenders of social norms who are like drill sergeants in a boot camp.

The patronage system still exists, though accompanied with secrecy and denial, but in the Greco-Roman world it was openly recognized and acknowledged as "the way things are done." In our time, we have tried to curb its ethical problems: nepotism, influence peddling, arbitrary cruelty by authorities, corruption of judges. But we are not being honest if we claim that the patronage system no longer exists. In fact, it is quite prevalent in churches; clergy who lack patrons may find themselves defenseless when injustice starts happening. To a large extent, the churches and the denominations are still run by personalities, not principles—it's *who* you know that matters, not what. This is the way of the world. It should not be the way of the churches.

We get some historical understanding of this if we look at the patronage system as it existed in Jesus' time. Everyone who lived in Greco-Roman societies understood the rules of patronage. Obligations and expectations were known more through oral tradition than written law until Roman law started to codify some of the rules.[27] The basic structure is binary. A powerful person (the patron) agrees to help a weaker person (the client) in return for certain favors. Powerful Roman citizens who wanted to get elected to one of the political assemblies, for instance, would build up a network of clients who "owed" them. When election time came, the client knew for whom they needed to vote, and possibly even to campaign.[28]

It is a system of doing favors, receiving favors, backing "our guy, right or wrong," and following the principle "you scratch my back, and I'll scratch yours." Common practices in such a system are giving gifts, returning favors, praising the patron, and keeping track of who owes you and whom you owe. Similar patterns appear in all human societies, since they derive from self-interested behaviors within societies where power is unevenly distributed (*every* society). They can be called reciprocity systems. Those of

27. Lampe, "Paul, Patrons, and Clients," 490.
28. Ibid., 491.

lower status are "obligated to reciprocate by conferring honour, praise, gratitude and loyalty to a patron or benefactor" who has assisted them.[29]

Bullying is a by-product of patronage. Patronage is about selfish grasping after power, which requires making allies and enemies; bullying arises as a way either to treat enemies (those in *other* patronage networks) or to coerce or humiliate one's own clients or those of a lower social status. Bullying weakens and possibly forces compliance from others. Bullies also feel powerful when they are humiliating others, so there is a psychological payoff.

Philosophers such as Plato, Seneca, Epictetus, and Cicero speak about patronage, largely because they are challenging the system and offering alternative sets of values.[30] In their different ways, they fight against cruel behavior. Seneca accepts that there is inequality in patronage, but he wants relationships to be handled gracefully and with consideration, without exploitation by patrons or ingratitude by clients.[31] Cicero tries to replace obligation with love, to reduce "the hope of gain" as a motivation,[32] even to replace patronage with friendship—a highly idealistic goal. Satirists like Martial and Juvenal made fun of both the groveling foolishness of clients and the arrogant selfishness of patrons.[33]

Characteristic of patronage systems is the competitiveness of those who seek to rise in status. Bullying by minor officials and mid-level managers was the subject of warnings by Greco-Roman writers, and of a parable of Jesus (Matt 18:23–35). In the parable, the mid-level person (actually, a slave) was despised because he was mean to those underneath him, and did not show the same mercy that the king had showed to him.

We should also point out that the patronage system would not work unless both parties got some benefit out of the arrangement.

29. Crook, *Reconceptualising Conversion*, 57, 64.

30. deSilva describes how Plato, Seneca, and Epictetus offer alternative values (*Despising Shame*, 82–99).

31. Rice, *Paul and Patronage*, 70.

32. Ibid., 59–62.

33. Ibid., 72–74.

In due course, clients will get some limited status and power by supporting a patron who has much greater status and power. It is a system of mutual, though unequal, reciprocity. Powerful patrons would have numerous clients, and those clients with less to offer would receive fewer benefits than those who could offer the patron more.

Even the gods were patrons and were approached through the patronage system. The gods expected to be shown "honor in the form of sacrifice and votive gifts"; clients were expected to show "indebted gratitude."[34] And the people who gave the gifts and built the shrines wanted the gods to do something in return. Characters in Homer let it be known that "the god should perform the service 'in order to' receive the offering."[35]

There is resistance to this self-serving thinking in the Bible, but some selfish religiosity can be seen as well. In Psalm 20, sacrificial gifts help get God to grant a person's desires: "May he remember all your offerings, and regard with favor your burnt sacrifices. May he grant you your heart's desire, and fulfill all your plans" (Ps 20:3–4). Psalm 116 suggests that the sacrifice is a payment to God for having received the latter's favor: "you have delivered my soul from death . . . What shall I return to the LORD for all his bounty to me? . . . I will pay my vows to the LORD in the presence of all his people . . . a thanksgiving sacrifice" (Ps 116:8, 12, 14, 17). The sacrificial vow is paid with maximum public exposure, inviting human and divine approval. Later psalmists are uncomfortable with the idea of God as a patron. Psalms 40:6; 50:9–13; and 51:16 frankly state that God does not want sacrifice, but the authors of Psalms 20 and 116 seem to be unaware of this critique.

Critics of Patronage

From the Torah, through the Wisdom literature, and into the Prophets and the New Testament, there are passages that resist the

34. Whitlark, *Enabling Fidelity to God*, 45, 19.

35. See Parker, "Pleasing Thighs," 108; he cites *Odyss.* 16.183–85 and *Iliad* 6:306–10, 10:291–92.

patronage system and its tendency to mistreat those who did not have a patron: "You shall not wrong or oppress a resident alien, for you were aliens in the land of Egypt. You shall not abuse any widow or orphan. If you do abuse them, when they cry out to me, I will surely heed their cry . . . and I will kill you with the sword" (Exod 22:21–24). God is the protector of the widow and orphan: those who have no husband or father to defend them, and who have no patron.

Sacrificial systems were largely a feature of patronage, with clients expressing their gratitude to their divine patrons. It makes sense that the critics of patronage should also criticize sacrificial offerings. Some psalmists and prophets mock sacrifice: "If I were hungry, I would not tell you, for the world and all that is in it is mine. Do I eat the flesh of bulls, or drink the blood of goats?" (Ps 50:12–13); "Will the Lord be pleased with thousands of rams, with tens of thousands of rivers of oil?" (Mic 6:7). Many theologians nowadays try to deny that there was any antisacrificial thrust in these prophets,[36] arguing that they only criticize sacrifice offered by unethical people. That was indeed the position of *some* prophets (Malachi, Ezekiel), but not of those who attack sacrifice *itself* (not just sacrificing by *sinners*): "Bringing offerings is futile" (Isa 1:13). There is a strong polemic against sacrifice itself: "Sacrifice and offering you do not desire. . . . For you have no delight in sacrifice" (Pss 40:6; 51:16).

Hosea *contrasts* love with sacrifice: "I desire steadfast love and not sacrifice" (Hos 6:6), a passage that is twice quoted by Jesus (Matt 9:13; 12:7). Jeremiah contrasts obedience and sacrifice, and attacks the idea that God established the sacrificial cult: "I did not speak to them or command them concerning burnt-offerings and sacrifices. But this command I gave them, 'Obey my voice'" (7:22–23; similarly, Amos 5:25). These prophets saw sacrifice as selfish, as a *show* of religiosity. But our greatest critics of patronage and selfish reciprocity are found in the New Testament.

36. Just one example: "It is unlikely that prophets or others would conceive of a religion . . . without sacrifice" (Eidevall, "The Role of Sacrificial Language," 53).

Jesus' Critique of Patronage

Jesus attacks the patronage system when he tells his disciples to invite the poor and the lame to a banquet, not relatives and rich neighbors who would be capable of repaying the favor. He says "when you give a banquet, invite the poor, the crippled, the lame, and the blind. And you will be blessed, because they cannot repay you" (Luke 14:13–14).

The patronage system always involves doing things for which you expect payback. It is all about social climbing and trying to get people to *owe* you. Both Jesus and Paul take aim at this motivation. Jesus offers something completely different from patronage when he tells the disciples not to "lord it over" others while claiming to be "benefactors. But not so with you; rather the greatest among you must become like the youngest, and the leader like one who serves" (Luke 22:25–26). He gave counterintuitive and paradoxical axioms: "the least among all of you is the greatest" (Luke 9:48); "The greatest among you will be your servant" (Matt 23:11). Jesus is redefining leadership, presenting servanthood as "an alternative to accepted patterns of leadership."[37] The Jesus method is incomprehensible to people operating under the spell of the patronage system, wherein one does not serve people who cannot repay. It seems to obliterate the obligations, separations, and distinctions upon which society depends.

Jesus proclaimed a "kingdom" that involved freedom from the usual social hierarchies imposed upon the poor, Gentiles, and women. He created a spiritual "family" of "brothers and sisters" who could eat together and pray together without class distinctions or gendered hierarchy. His "provocative practice of open table fellowship also obliterated boundaries based on impurity, socioeconomic class distinctions, and ethnicity."[38]

Even more remarkable was his attitude toward children, his open invitation to them, and his using them as a symbol for

37. Yoder, *Politics of Jesus*, 46. Jesus uplifts those who are subordinate in society (Yoder, *Politics of Jesus*, 178).

38. Talbott, *Jesus, Paul, and Power*, 59.

reception of the kingdom of God (Mark 10:14–16; Matt 19:14). But his statements about children are not just symbolic. He really wants children to be respected, sternly warning his disciples not to "put a stumbling block before one of these little ones" or to "despise one of these little ones" (Matt 18:6, 10). He even identifies himself with children when he says "Whoever welcomes one such child in my name welcomes me" (Matt 18:5).

Jesus "was indignant" with the disciples for dismissing children (Mark 10:14). He commanded his disciples to change their attitudes toward children. This is supported by his teachings about God, as in the Prodigal Son story, where the "father" is extraordinarily forgiving. In those days, fatherly authority over the child was emphasized, but Jesus stressed fatherly love. Walter Wink puts it this way: "In the new family of Jesus there are only children, no patriarchs."[39] For his day, Jesus' respect for children was even more remarkable than his respect for servants, foreigners, and women. It is radically nonhierarchic.

And yet, his parables are populated with patrons (sometimes kindly, sometimes stern or demanding) and clients or servants (of all kinds: loyal, shrewd, or foolish). He told realistic stories, but with moral lessons; using characters and situations that people would readily recognize. The parable of the Unforgiving Servant teaches that a servant whose patron had forgiven his debt was wrong to bully others ("seizing him by the throat . . . threw him into prison," Matt 18:28, 30).[40]

There is plenty of patronage in today's churches, and patrons can be bullies (so can clients, jostling for position in competition with other clients). The problem is more severe in denominations with an episcopal (bishop-run) structure. The bishop is the chief patron, but the patron with whom most ministers must deal is the area minister or district superintendent. Patronage spawns many evils, such as careerism (putting one's career ahead of everything

39. Wink, *Engaging the Powers*, 119.

40. Shockingly, the servant is handed over to be tortured in 18:34–35. There are much harsher images of judgment in Matthew than in the other Gospels. This tells us more about *Matthew's* views than about Jesus'.

else, ahead of principle, ahead of justice). The careerist may know that the district superintendent is a bully, but be unwilling to say or do anything about it, not wanting to jeopardize his or her standing with the DS. Thusly do clergy often stay silent, even when they know wrongdoing is taking place. No careerist wants to stick her neck out. Thus, abusive leaders are able to stay in power.

Paul's Answer to Patronage

The Apostle Paul's churches were the laboratories in which he attempted to instill a different standard of values than what was common in either Gentile or Jewish societies. Consider, as though reading it for the first time, how radical this saying is: "There is no longer Jew or Greek, there is no longer slave or free, there is no longer male and female, for all of you are one in Christ Jesus" (Gal 3:28). We will fail to appreciate how daring this statement was if we do not notice that it applies a standard of values completely at odds with the patronage system. Ethnicity, class, and gender are all made irrelevant.

And yet, Paul uses the logic of patronage in exercising his authority over his churches, even while he is trying to remove the barriers of social status. He uses his status as founder of the Co- rinthian congregation to criticize some Corinthians' behavior at Eucharistic meals, where some have food and some do not, and the wealthy "humiliate those who have nothing" (1 Cor 11:22). Paul feels strongly that the pride of the feasters is a betrayal of the gospel. But he is only able to get them to change by asserting his paternalistic authority over them, so there is a certain irony and complexity in Paul's strategy. We need to notice both aspects of Paul's position, his advocacy of radically egalitarian treatment of others *and* his assertion of authority over his congregations—even a *teaching* authority over a congregation he did *not* found (in Rome).

Paul also uses the logic of patronage with Philemon, one of his converts. The Epistle of Philemon is perhaps the most underap- preciated book in the Bible, as it shows how a genuine application of the Christian principle of brotherhood leads logically to the freeing of slaves. Paul is trying to convince one of his clients (the slave owner Philemon) to free another of his clients (the slave Onesimus), so that Onesimus may return to Philemon "no longer as a slave, but . . . a beloved brother" (Phlm 16). He bluntly reminds Philemon that he is Paul's spiritual client: "I say nothing about your owing me even your own self" (v. 19), that is, his very soul! He has the right "to command you," but he prefers that Philemon's act "be voluntary" (vv. 8, 14). Paul is the patron, asking a client to obey, and he is "confident of your obedience" (v. 21).

So Jesus and Paul both use images and terminology of patronage because that is what people knew, and they would recognize the image. But they set out to present a different scale of values, wherein one does good without seeking reward, "your alms may be done in secret" (Matt 6:4), where we act with "a spirit of gentleness. . . . Bear one another's burdens" and yet where each one is responsible for his or her own obligations, "for all must carry their own loads" (Eph 6:1–2, 5).

So—is bullying caused by sheer competition and the desire to get ahead, or by a herd mentality among entrenched groups in the church, or possibly by group aggression directed against a single victim, or by the perpetuation of cruelties suffered in childhood, or even by the survival of the patronage system? Yes! All of these are factors that can lead to bullying in churches. Each pastor, each Christian, needs to develop a synthetic method for coming to an understanding of the causes and methods of bullying, and to build up some experience with psychologically wise, socially informed, and Christ-inspired responses to bullying. Some solutions will be discussed in chapters 5 and 6, but first it is necessary to look at some specific bullying behaviors in churches.

4 – Bullying Behaviors and Targets

THERE ARE CERTAIN COMMON patterns of behavior that we should examine: rationalizing, anti-intellectualism, bullying by the pastor, and bullying *of* the pastor. But there is something that must be mentioned first, to remove a common misconception about bullies: "'The myth that the bully has low self-esteem has largely been debunked in recent years"; they are "socially adept"; they simply want "to increase their own social status."[1] To some degree, it is naïve goodwill that has led people to think that bullies have low self-esteem, and that all they need is some help with it. Unfortunately, the problem is more severe than that; it involves actual *sin*: ill will toward others.

Rationalization

Not many people like to think of themselves as bullies. There are a number of ways that bullies rationalize how they treat their targets: "they brought this on themselves"; "he needs to toughen up"; "she shouldn't act so weird"; "somebody needs to show him"; "it's just a joke, she shouldn't take it so seriously." Some of these rationalizations masquerade as being instructional or helpful. After all, the reason that people rationalize is to justify (to themselves and to others) behaviors that would otherwise seem unjustifiable. There is often a certain amount of dishonesty in the rationalizing process;

---

1. Whitson, *Eight Keys to End Bullying*, 13.

the degree to which this dishonesty is *conscious*, however, can vary greatly. Some school age bullies rationalize that the "strong" are better than "the weak," and are *meant* to dominate them, "because that is true in their families."[2] Some bullies even rationalize that their "victims actually enjoyed being bullied. . . . 'If he didn't like it, he'd quit acting queer, and then we wouldn't pick on him.'"[3] They blame the victim ("He asked for it").[4]

In fact, the motivation is usually more destructive than the bully wishes to admit. Bullying may be meant to humiliate a subordinate, to disempower a nonconformist, to take down a leader, to shame an outsider, or to assert one's own power and status in the eyes of beholders. Bullying is an assertion of power. The bully could be trying to ingratiate him- or herself with the ruling group, acting upon what s/he thinks are the attitudes of the ruling clique or gang. The bully could also be part of a minority that is trying to grab power, and thinks that this goal may be achieved by appearing "tougher" or "smarter" than the targeted individual. Language that the bully uses can communicate contempt for a certain style or set of values: "sissy," "fundamentalist," "whiner," "bleeding heart," although we cannot always assume that the criticism is honest or sincere. The clever bully may well be choosing whatever accusation he thinks will be effective, and avoiding using labels that would reveal the bully's own bias or unfairness. As with con artists, the most effective bullies are also the most dishonest.

It is important to distinguish physical bullying from mental bullying. Physical bullies are the more aggressive type; they have little or no empathy for others. The mental bullies are more socially advanced; that is, they tend to have above average "emotional intelligence," the ability to read others' emotions.[5] Unfortunately, they also have very good manipulative skills.

Bullying can happen within the vertical hierarchies of denominations. District superintendents, regional supervisors, district

---

2. Hunt, *Bullying*, 42, 44.

3. Orpinas and Horne, *Bullying Prevention*, 68.

4. Ibid., 69.

5. Rigby, *New Perspectives on Bullying*, 133.

committees, vestries, and pastors can choose to bully someone of lower status, to aggressively assert their power. Various motivations can underlie the bullying: to silence criticism or complaint; to discipline or punish or compel submission; to squelch ambition or to clear a way for someone else's ambition. The bullying person can use various different rationalizations to deny to himself or herself that s/he is engaging in bullying.

Bullying or mocking can be meant to suppress someone's creativity or theology. New ideas can be very threatening to religious authorities. We can start with the example of the prophet Amos, who aroused the resentment of the chief priest Amaziah, who complained to "King Jeroboam of Israel, saying 'Amos has conspired against you in the very center of the house of Israel; the land is not able to bear all his words,'" and then told Amos, "O seer, go, flee away . . . never again prophesy at Bethel" (Amos 7:10, 12–13). Similarly, the Sanhedrin felt threatened by Jesus, and appealed to the highest political authority (Pontius Pilate) to have him permanently silenced. It is likely that the members of the Sanhedrin applied the same rationalizations for their behavior as Amaziah did: that they were not defending their own interests in a cowardly manner, but were standing up for the nation that was somehow threatened by an individual's critical voice. Caiaphas claimed to be defending "the whole nation" when he said it was acceptable for that one man to die (John 11:50).

Many people, when confronted with their bad behavior, have ready excuses for it: "you just weren't listening, so I had to say it louder." "There are people in this church who say you are not nice to the volunteers." Bossy pastors can also come up with excuses: "Stop thinking you're so important. I can't drop what I'm doing to attend to your needs."

Anti-Intellectualism

Sometimes bullying is a way of suppressing or discrediting someone who raises uncomfortable questions, who asks people to rethink their opinions. The crowd can feel very threatened by someone who challenges the consensus, especially if it is an un-examined consensus. Few things provoke the rage of lazy-minded people as much as being told to *think*.

Jesus certainly asked people to think and to change. It was the sycophantic clients, taking a cue from their leaders, who complained to Pilate that "he stirs up the people by teaching . . . per-verting the people," and who refused to listen to Pilate's suggestion that he was innocent (Luke 23:5, 14–23). Christians have some-times been the worst hypocrites on this score. Catholic leaders lured the Reformer Jan Hus to the Council of Constance, and then had him killed. Protestants have not been innocent of violence: Anabaptists and Unitarians were killed by Lutheran and Calvinist authorities. No denomination has had a monopoly on "Christian" violence. The suppression of ideas happens today in the churches in a different way, with force that is aimed at destroying someone's reputation and career instead of their body. But the same process of slander, conspiracy, backstabbing, and suppression goes on now as in the times when the churches actually killed people. Now they just kill hope, and justice, and trust.

Bullying might be more common in churches on the far Left or far Right, where there are accepted doctrines and positions, and other doctrines or viewpoints that are vilified. Bullying thrives in *any* extremist atmosphere. Whenever there is strong pressure to think alike or speak alike, anyone who retains unique qualities or viewpoints is in danger. Most people find it hard enough even in the best of environments to be fully tolerant and respectful of those who think differently from themselves, but in a totalitarian group conformity is expected, and dissent is not even honored with lip service. However, bullying can also happen in any "mod-erate" church, if hypocrisy reigns.

Our mechanized and complex culture tends to crush unique-ness, so it becomes all the more necessary that we work to preserve the human element, and that we resist the pressure to suppress individuality. Just as there needed to be Jews and Greeks, rich and poor in Paul's churches, so now there need to be conservatives and liberals, rich and poor and struggling in *our* churches. If our spirituality is not able to transcend our identity politics, then it is not spiritual at all. If we are not being challenged to love those who *differ* from ourselves and who do not share all of our opinions, then we are not stretching mentally or spiritually, and we are not really the church of God. One should meet and love people at church that one would not meet and love in one's social circles. If church does not ask you to stretch spiritually, it is not doing its job. And this includes the need to allow space for those who think ahead, who ask troubling questions, who even have innovative and unusual ideas. Every advance in human thinking was originally perceived as strange or unorthodox. Of course, most strange or unorthodox views will turn out *not* to be an advance, but we don't always know that in advance! Further, there is a value in individual uniqueness that needs to be appreciated, whether or not the person is going to lead an advance in civilization.

There is a bias held by many Christians (including many pastors) that intellectuals and scholars cannot make good pastors. When pastors aim to keep their congregations infantile and to keep Christian education at a very elementary level, then this bias becomes a self-fulfilling prophecy. Is it right to assume that Christians do not want their brains taxed, or lack the intelligence to tax them in the first place? What about loving God with our whole *minds*, not just with our whole hearts and souls? This does not mean that education will be quick and easy, but when has a good education *ever* been quick or easy? It is hard work, and requires persistence from both teachers and students (and every teacher must remember to be a perpetual student).

It is not possible to raise the educational level of a congregation quickly, but it *is* possible to raise it *gradually*, and that is a pastor's obligation. Pastors who deliberately keep their flock ignorant have betrayed the pastoral responsibility to teach (Matt 28:20; Acts 2:42; 1 Cor 12:28; etc.).

Bullying by the Pastor

The pastor's position carries enormous power. The person in this position is authorized to speak about God, the soul, sin, salvation, and eternity. What other profession in society is given such ideological authority? Further, the pastor is more or less the CEO of the local church, sitting on most or all committees, helping choose the lay leaders for the congregation, and supervising assistant clergy or students undergoing supervised ministry assignments. A pastor who is inclined to be bossy or impatient will have many opportunities to demonstrate these behaviors, and often the people around the pastor do not know how to kindly but honestly critique this behavior and guide him or her on a more Christian path. "Yes-men" and other spiritually weak follower types are not going to help the pastor see what s/he is doing that is hurtful.

Unfortunately, many churchgoers show signs of arrested development. Many churchgoers are "joiners," people who lean toward conformism and conventional morality. They are not necessarily "yes-men," but they may not be capable of calmly and directly challenging someone in a leadership position. It is no mistake that Jesus referred to disciples as sheep (especially John 21:15–17; but also John 10:4–16, 26–27; Mark 6:34; Luke 15:4; etc.). Even the word "pastor" refers to someone who guides sheep. But this image is not meant to enforce a permanent infantile state. An enlightened pastor should educate his/her flock, to raise the level of spiritual wisdom and responsibility. There is a growth and progress mandate that applies to all aspects of our spiritual life: "be perfect, therefore, as your heavenly Father is perfect" (Matt 5:48). This refers to an endless *perfecting* process, not to *being* perfect at any given time, which is not possible for us here on earth. It is always the responsibility of the more educated and mature people to help along those less educated or mature. It seems obvious (to me) that pastors should be well educated and mature, and that seminaries and churches should have high standards for this. Unfortunately, all too often, "the violent take it by force" (Matt 11:12)—and that is *within* the church (and in the seminary)!

A bossy pastor can get used to having his or her way on any and all issues, becoming increasingly impatient and rude, and the congregation can get used to it being that way. When someone pulls aside a longtime member and questions the pastor's disrespectful behavior, the longtime member might say, "You know how the pastor is. S/he is in charge. What can we do? Do *you* want to confront him/her? *I'm* not going to step into that! You're on your own."

Congregations and pastors can get stuck in habit. The excuse "s/he's always been this way" is used as though it were a legitimate reason to say nothing. "Gentleness and self-control" are important fruits of the spirit (Gal 5:23), and a pastor who lacks them is lacking in maturity. Bullying is a transgression. We can apply Paul's advice even if the transgressor is the pastor: "restore such a one in a spirit of gentleness" (Gal 6:1). We should be, "with patience, bearing with one another in love, making every effort to maintain the unity of the Spirit in the bond of peace" (Eph 4:2–3).

I heard a story of a church volunteer who needed to leave her youth director position so she could go back to college. Using guilt, the pastor told her she could not leave. The pastor then got the young people in the group to pressure her to stay, and to repeat his allegations that she would be abandoning the youth if she left. Fortunately, she decided to walk away from that abusive situation, hopefully without any guilt. The pastor was using guilt to manipulate her; we need to recognize and repudiate such manipulation. Knock the dust of that place off your sandals! (Matt 10:14).

Bullying the Pastor

Sometimes an opposite phenomenon is observed: groups within the congregation can gang up on a pastor and make either direct or indirect attacks. Indirect attacks are probably more common. These takes the form of complaining, passing on the complaints of others, sometimes magnifying what is passed on, and enjoying the "juicy" details that one is hearing or passing on. Gossip is a spirit poison in many churches. Before long, an antipastor clique can form, which starts describing its opinions as "everybody's" opinions: "everybody is sick of the pastor's choice of hymns," for example, or "nobody agrees with the pastor's vision for the church." Such comments will be kept partially hidden at first. But when the group knows it has the numbers, it will bring the criticism or negativity out into the open. They need to be reminded that there is "nothing secret that will not become known" (Matt 10:26).

Others may never share their criticisms, but only operate behind the scenes, complaining about the pastor and seeking to find fellow complainers, a behavior known as triangulation. The pastor may never know that the individual has a negative attitude, but will hear from others what "people in the church" are saying. Sometimes the person saying these things is using cowardly indirection to express his or her own opinion; no wonder Paul was concerned about the "hostility, slander, gossip" in the congregation at Corinth (2 Cor 12:20 ESV). How can a pastor respond to complaints that are never made openly in a responsible manner or in an appropriate forum?

This does not mean that all dissent or criticism is bullying. I only use the word "bullying" if there is grasping for power and an edge of cruelty. If a group seeks to do damage to a pastor's standing and pursues this goal with cruelty, then their actions can indeed be called "bullying." In any church there need to be opportunities to openly discuss policies (the church council, consistory, or vestry) as well as another place to bring up more personal complaints, usually within a staff-parish relations committee. Further, there need to be grievance procedures (see "Grievance Procedures" in chapter 5). But there should be no place for backstabbing, triangulating, or slander.

It is God's will that the bully should undergo a change of heart: "I will remove from your body the heart of stone and give you a heart of flesh. I will put my spirit within you" (Ezek 36:26–27). Unfortunately, most people with a heart of stone will reject this difficult path, because it involves the painful effort of honest self-examination and submission to a higher power. They *do* look to a certain power: the power of being part of a gang or cabal that can do damage to a pastor who they decide is of the wrong gender or has the wrong style, or who has spoken out against certain behaviors in the church.

We also have pastors being bullied by their clergy superintendent or supervisor, an especially disgraceful but all-too-common behavior. Some superintendents will make common cause with complainers who wish to triangulate against the pastor, seizing upon any complaint that is convenient for their own purposes, including their quest for adulation.

Do certain unprincipled district superintendents and spineless bishops side with the backstabbers in the churches because the latter give money? "The customer is always right" may be a common adage, but it is not a biblical principle. Denominational leaders should know better than to allow people to triangulate against a pastor, avoid talking with the pastor about their complaints, or undermine the church's established procedures for discussing disagreements and hearing complaints. Even secular society does not think that slander and bullying are perfectly fine, and many secular employers strive to prevent these shameful behaviors. Why does the church often lag behind the secular workplace? We need to take ethics seriously. Of course, many superintendents *do*. Superintendents and bishops are individuals; not all show the moral weaknesses that I and others have seen.

We should learn to stand up to unethical behavior. It should be part of our value system that we seek to "rescue the weak and the needy; deliver them from the hand of the wicked" (Ps 82:4). We should be "building up the neighbor" (Rom 15:2), defending him from harm, especially within the church. This is one of the neglected meanings of "bear one another's burdens" (Gal 6:2), which most people seem to interpret strictly in economic terms. What about the burden of having one's spirit crushed by backstabbing and lies? "Healing words give life, but dishonest words crush the spirit" (Prov 15:4 NCV). How many pastors are praying "save me from all my pursuers, and deliver me, or like a lion they will tear me apart" (Ps 7:1–2)?

5 - Preventive Practices in Churches

BY REMOVING THE VEIL of silence from the subject of bullying, we can begin to talk about it in the churches, and discuss exactly *how* we would like the ethics of love and respect to be practiced. Do we want to form prayer and study groups that work intensely on relationships within small groups, and, after trust has been built and understanding gained, combine the groups so that the whole congregation is involved in the same discussion? Or do we want to let ministry unfold in its usual manner, but be very diligent about relationship processes for handling conflicts? With the former approach, concentrated work on relationships would be ongoing; with the latter such work would only happen when problems occur. In either case, the pastor would be wise to include the principles of relationship building and showing respect in his or her sermons. The need for a higher awareness of relationship issues is a spiritual need, and thus becomes a necessary topic in pastoral teaching.

There are a number of ways to structure the work on relationships, so I will not say much more about structure. I will be focusing on developing an underlying ethos, and learning how to recognize healthy motivations, values, and communication techniques.

An Ethic of Respect

This section could have been titled "Teaching about Respect," but I instead wanted to emphasize that no amount of teaching will do any good if that ethic is not internalized by rank and file members of the congregation. Unless a real spiritual ethos is operative, genuine conflict resolution will not take place. But if a sufficient percentage of the congregation genuinely wants honest and respectful relationships, this desirable goal can be realized, although it may take time and effort. Healthy ministry must be built on respectful and positive principles and a real attention to relationships.

Along with the ethic of respect needs to go a technique of wise communication. If you feel hurt or disrespected by something someone in the church said, you can try to tell the person this, but it is best to use "I" statements instead of saying what "you" or "they" did. For instance, rather than saying "you insulted me" or "you were rude," try saying "I felt put down by that remark." Whatever the other's intention was, you can definitely state how you felt; another can hardly refute how you *felt*. If the other person is completely indifferent to how you feel, or says you are stupid for feeling that way, then you know you are dealing with a genuinely disrespectful person, and that you cannot expect much in the way of sensitivity or fairness from him or her. You can also draw attention to the fact that you are using "I" statements in hopes that the other will recognize that you are trying to encourage a nonjudgmental conversation in which everyone's feelings are respected. If the person supports that effort, then both parties will benefit from the conversation, both may become better listeners, and no one becomes overwhelmingly angry or threatened.

I want to rephrase a point I made in the second chapter ("The Effect of the Jesus Ethic"), that the gospel is meant to restore self-respect to those who have been hurt in that area, and restrain self-regard in those who already have plenty of it. Jesus said "take heart" to the wounded, "blessed are the pure of heart" to the neglected, but "woe" to heartless leaders, and "depart from me" to those whose deeds did not match their words. He knew when someone needed a word of encouragement, or when a person needed a rebuke.

Jesus defends those who are unfairly criticized by saying "let her alone" (Mark 14:6). He stands up for people, he builds up the downcast, he ignores cultic impurity, gender, profession, and nationality. He speaks well of shunned women, tax collectors, Syrians, and Samaritans. Who are the Samaritans or the shunned persons in *our* circles? Perhaps the hostility is not along racial or gender lines, but is directed against nonconformists, "geeks," or "nerds." We must articulate the belief that all people are children of the Most High, and worthy of respect.

We should follow Jesus' example in honoring persons who have values and good intentions. We need to learn to recognize them, sometimes to name them so that the person hears what values the other recognizes. Sometimes a person's good intentions are hard to read, which might mean that one's powers of discernment are limited and one needs to suspend judgment until more data is available; or, it might mean one is having to deal with a narcissist, whose intentions are entirely selfish.

We can reach someone who has values and good will, but not a person with narcissistic personality disorder. When Jesus spoke about forgiveness, he was not recommending behavior that makes one a doormat, but that makes one the master of the situation. A forgiving attitude can sometimes help to expose the rationalizations or dishonesty of bullies, but will usually not cause them to have an attack of conscience (though we wish it would).

Finally, pastors must engage in a program of self-care, no matter what is going on in their churches. Rediger draws a pyramid of five "spiritual disciplines," with the broad base being the most important and most frequently needed: the practice of "worship . . . silence, praise, and individual as well as corporate communion with God."[1] Rediger distinguishes worship from prayer. I want to expand his point about worship, and combine it with something written by William Hocking a century ago. Worship is the essential basic spiritual practice that every pastor needs; worship is where

1. Rediger, *Clergy Killers*, 177, 179.

we forget ourselves (to the degree that's possible) and turn to God in calmness. Worship is different from prayer, which is self-interested, serious, and concerned; worship is God-interested, serene, and conjoined. Worship does not appear until prayer subsides and "gives way to passivity in the discovery of an object of *effortless appreciation.*"[2] Worship is always a pleasurable and reenergizing experience, whereas prayer may sometimes be painful and tiring. Prayer can leave us frustrated, but worship reminds us that we rely on a power not our own. And "it is only the true worshipper who can find the world genuinely lovable."[3]

Valuing Differences

One of the long-term effects of Christian socialization has been to increase the appreciation for human differences, individuality, and diversity. At one time, this involved love and understanding between Jews and Gentiles; now it tends to mean meeting and appreciating people from different ethnic backgrounds, economic levels, and of a different sexual orientation than one's own. Society at large is coming to recognize basic sexual orientation as something that is to be accepted and not repressed. Some churches still follow the repression of same-sex orientation, pointing to Leviticus for justification, even though they do not share the worldview of Leviticus, nor its view of purity, nor do they follow its other rules. Other churches do not follow Leviticus, but they struggle to articulate their reasons for not following the Bible literally.

I think this will help: The heart of our religion is not the literal word of Scripture but the person and spirit of Jesus; it is "a revelation of Jesus Christ" (Gal 1:2). God shines in our hearts, and gives us "knowledge of the glory of God in the face of Jesus Christ" (2 Cor 4:6). *That* is our source of truth and our center of spirituality. Christianity is not doctrine or ritual; Christianity is Christ. There are enormous differences of viewpoint and theology

2. Hocking, *Meaning of God*, 422.
3. Ibid., 439.

within Scripture, and not all passages are helpful toward the formation of a Jesus-based philosophy. Sharon Baker recommends reading Scripture through "the Jesus lens. . . . , interpreting these texts through the lens of Jesus' life and teachings."[4]

As Christians have reflected on their societies down through time, Christian social morals have changed again and again. Marriage morals and customs have been in a state of continual change for several centuries. Theologian Adrian Thatcher insists "The teaching of Jesus supports whatever arrangements best assist the thriving of children,"[5] and that means a committed marriage, but there are many reasons now for "extending the rite and the right of marriage to couples of the same sex."[6] This should be more courageously and calmly discussed in our society and in our churches.

A perennial challenge in any church (actually, in any group where beliefs and values are prominent) is to learn to achieve some degree of spiritual connection and alliance with people who *think* or *believe* differently than oneself. This may be a bigger challenge than just learning to get along with people of different classes and ethnicities. Valuing differences needs to mean valuing each person's individuality, even that of the nonconformist, the critic, or the one who asks uncomfortable questions. It must mean learning to appreciate the people who have historically been made the targets of group bullying, even scapegoats for the violence of a community that feels threatened.

The nonconformist is the most likely person to get bullied in any society, but from their ranks come the great thinkers, reformers, even scientists and teachers. The creativity of the nonconformist is *needed.* Many of the greatest nonconformists have made great contributions to society before they were silenced: great questioners like Socrates, moral critics like John the Baptist, innovative scientists like Galileo. The philosophers of Athens might have become a more honest and open lot if they had allowed Socrates to continue to criticize their shallow reasoning. Jewish leaders might

4. Baker, *Razing Hell*, 59–60, 64.

5. Thatcher, *Theology and Families*, 127.

6. Ibid., 137.

have curbed their selfish appetites if John had been allowed to live. Even more astounding to contemplate is what Jesus might have been able to accomplish if the religious leaders of his culture had not conspired against him.

The battles that go on in churches nowadays may have nothing to do with life and death, but they are fought with as much fervor as though they did. But a pastor who wishes to inculcate the practice of valuing differences by bringing in different liturgical forms may be in for a surprise. Some of the fiercest church battles were provoked by changes in liturgy. It is advisable to preach about the proposed change before implementing it. Even that is far from a guarantee that changes in liturgy will be tolerated. Pastors need to be cautious about introducing changes in those areas where conservatism is most strongly entrenched.

Teaching and preaching are of primary importance. Preaching about the valuing of differences should be done thoughtfully and with a view to really helping people understand. A moral victory has been won if the congregation has learned to respect and be curious about other cultures and other branches of Christianity. Intellectual curiosity is a great stimulus of interreligious dialogue.

Training Ourselves

Certain behaviors need to be reinforced through repeated teaching, posted signs, and reinforcement in conversation, so that they eventually become habits. They are not habits to start with, or such measures would not be necessary.

One group that has been working on a declared policy against bullying is the Southampton District of the British Methodist Church, arising out of the Basingstoke Circuit Meeting's proposal for a "Positive Working Together" approach. It states "the Methodist Church does not currently have a shared understanding of or sufficient ways of dealing with issues relating to the behaviour of church members towards each other, including in respect to bullying, harassment and dealing with disagreements."[7] The group recommends a fourfold approach: having an anti-bullying policy, working on a statement of "shared commitment" for dealing respectfully with disagreements, forming a network of "support for people encountering difficult relationships in churches . . . but not for taking sides," and training for church members and leaders that explains the other three parts of the process and works on "how to constructively deal with negative behaviour and with power issues." The conference authorities reacted positively to the suggestion, and will be making a report to the 2015 conference.

As declared in the first sentence of Basingstoke's statement, we cannot just assume that everyone in the church has a shared understanding of what is and is not acceptable behavior. Denominational leadership needs to study and discuss the problem of bullying; only in this way will denominations, or regions within the denominations, experience a consciousness raising about this serious ethical problem.

Several ingredients in church practice need to work together to instill the ethics of respect and nonbullying. Educational courses in small groups would be one possible, but not absolutely necessary, ingredient. Preaching against bullying and in favor of respectfulness seems to be an absolutely necessary element; it is part of the gospel itself. Committees or research groups that look into bullying would be an option. Posting signs and slogans would be an option. Each pastor and each congregation need to address this, hopefully artfully, and not just as though promoting a new dogma. The beauty and thoughtfulness with which an idea is presented are just as important as the truth content of the idea. What is important is that there be consistent opposition to bullying, from the small group level up to the denominational leadership.

Teaching against bullying is now *essential*. I have some passion on this subject, since I have been bullied. It is crucial that church leaders be people who are honest and just. It is not enough that they see partially, or that they can dimly discern when someone is being treated unjustly. They need to be people who are repulsed by

7. Memorial 28, "Memorial to the Methodist Conference of 2013."

injustice and lies. Christians need to be people who are genuinely devoted to truth, and you cannot say you are devoted to truth if you do not *hate* lies. We must stop being so indulgent of liars in the church. It is a hateful and harmful behavior that does damage to people and to the liar's own relationship to God: "No one who utters lies shall continue in my presence" (Ps 101:7). Those who listen to lies are as bad as those who tell them: "An evildoer listens to wicked lips; and a liar gives heed to a mischievous tongue" (Prov 17:4). This tells us that liars *listen* to lies, are *drawn* to lies, not just that they tell them!

We need Christians who not only *claim* to love truth and justice, but who demonstrate that they are repulsed by cruelty and outraged by lies. There is really no room for neutrality on this issue. If you are not repulsed by lies, then you are probably complicit with them. Another area where there is no neutrality is on the need for honest goodwill between clergy and congregation. Terry Teykl has written a book that stresses the need for congregations to pray for their clergy: "A pastor not prayed for is preyed upon. . . . Since pastors do spiritual work, they need prayer for spiritual anointing. . . . You need to begin to organize a prayer force for your shepherd."[8] Obviously, the pastor also needs to pray for the congregation. Honest prayer will support goodwill in the community. It should be obvious that one cannot pray an *honest* prayer and still wish evil upon the one prayed for.

We also need to face the fact that narcissistic antagonists and calculating clergy killers "will not yield to kindness or appeasement," and that we are using the wrong methods by "trying to mollify them, and trying to negotiate with them."[9] Rediger recommends "interventions to isolate and disable them,"[10] which assumes, of course, that the church leadership is able to recognize the inappropriateness of an antagonist's actions. We have a very different problem when some of the church leaders *are* the antagonists, and the other leaders indulge them, refusing to notice mis-

8. Teykl, *Preyed On or Prayed For*, 119, 79, 98.

9. Rediger, *Clergy Killers*, 123.

10. Ibid. I will address the issue of isolating an evildoer in the next section.

behavior. When the church leaders are *enablers* of bad behavior, there is no solution. Slander and bullying will rule the day.

The leadership of the church needs to be sane, mature, and responsible enough to be able to take action against bullies, which will be discussed in the next section.

Grievance Procedures and Disfellowshipping

Only in a church that takes ethics seriously will there be a grievance procedure that can be expected to function justly, and not as a way to sweep problems under the rug or to impose politically correct slogans upon problems.

It is important to remember that bullying is not a stand-alone phenomenon. It is related to values, loyalties, and desires. A person may intend to defend certain customs or responsibilities, but may do so without much empathy for those who come into his or her sightes. This will give rise to conflicts. In trying to mediate these disputes, it may be helpful to draw attention to values, to ask people to articulate what values they are attempting to defend. This can lead to a broadening of understanding between the disputing parties. It also may expose whose motives are more honest and selfless, whose are more devious and selfish, and whose motives are mixed. Even the mediator may learn something unpleasant about him- or herself. But if there is mercy, generosity, and honest intention, the mediator and the disputing parties will all benefit. It is important, however, to recognize when one of the disputants is being dishonest or ill-willed, when s/he does not actually desire reconciliation or mutual understanding, when revenge and blame have become ends in themselves. The honest and forgiving party should not be asked to bear part of the blame when the other party is motivated wholly by hate and acting only out of cruelty, with no desire for mutuality. There is no guaranteed method for insuring that mediators will strike the right balance, but we can at least articulate what we would like them to notice. We would like them to be able to discern when one party is honestly seeking resolution and reconciliation, and the other is not.

When a grievance procedure is in place and when the church takes it seriously, then the motivation of the bully or antagonist, who does not have an honest grievance but only wants to do harm, will become obvious to clear-thinking people. The bully will either not want to use the grievance procedure, or will use it insincerely, in a way that will be apparent to any observer with a clear sense of justice. The bully will eventually show his or her hand through the inconsistency or one-sidedness of his or her complaint, through impatience with the procedure's gradual and thoroughgoing pace, or through contempt for the stated aim of reconciliation. But this does not happen if there is not a social procedure for handling the grievance. The *procedures* of justice are an important part of justice. The procedure will tend to shine a light upon everyone's motives. This does not happen, at least not as clearly, if no grievance procedure exists. So what happens next?

Clearly, a dishonest person needs to awaken to the evil of what s/he is doing, but that may take a lifetime, and the church has a right to take action to defend its people against that person's destructiveness. One might ask, "What should the procedure be with those narcissists who cannot be reached?" Another might ask, "What if I've already gone the second mile with someone, but they are more dishonest than ever? It feels like I've forgiven him seventy times seven." Well, Jesus gave us a procedure, a three-step plan for dealing with a church member who "sins against you" (Matt 18:15), where there is real evildoing against oneself. I will paraphrase the three-step procedure: a) approach the offender directly and try to get him/her to see that what s/he did was wrong; b) if that fails, approach with one or two friends and try to reason; c) if that fails, take your complaint to the congregation and let them do the confronting, "and if the offender refuses to listen even to the church, let such a one be to you as a Gentile and a tax collector" (Matt 18:17). Of course, in Matthew's community, what that means is "let him be banished from the congregation."

There is a *need* for a procedure for disfellowshipping—*banning*—such persons from the congregation, but it cannot happen if the congregation is weak, confused, complicit in the bullying and the slandering, or frightened to take any action. Notice that the Jesus procedure does not concern cases where there are two viewpoints that each have some legitimacy. There are other venues and procedures for such cases. The Jesus procedure concerns cases of genuine sinning.

Each denomination has a judicial procedure that bears some resemblance to the technique Jesus outlined, or at least to steps two and three of the process, but it may also resemble mediation procedures designed to get two parties to understand each other. Assessing these procedures lies beyond the scope of this book. I will assume that there are decent and functional procedures in every church, but that dishonesty, corruption, and selfishness may prevent them from functioning the way they should.

The Gospel passage is clear enough, and I will stay focused on it, and I ask whether *your* church is able to practice it. The Jesus procedure for handling ethical conflicts in the church assumes a church community with a certain level of maturity and responsibility in the leadership *and* the membership. Unfortunately, our churches do not always measure up. Sometimes one who attempts to implement the Jesus procedure will just have to proceed as far as one *can* with it. A community that is unable to practice the Jesus procedure, that cannot recognize the issues or act responsibly, is one that is deeply unhealthy and dysfunctional. It is not practicing the gospel. If one recognizes this, one should probably leave that community. Theoretically, one could stay and become a prophetic voice against the betrayal of the gospel, but what effect can one really have as a lone voice for truth when one has no coworkers for truth? Really practicing the gospel means working *with* others to fulfill the will of God. When we pray "your will be done," it is in the context of a corporate prayer to "*our* Father" (Matt 6:9). The gospel involves collaboration.

6 – Protecting Vulnerable People

THERE IS NO SPECIAL demographic of vulnerable people or non-vulnerable people. Anyone can be vulnerable to being harmed by slander, cruelty, and lies. But there is a need for some attention to particular groups that commonly suffer bullying. First of all, there are children and teenagers. Children, even in Christian settings, can be very cruel to other children. As young people become conscious of social status and power, they can very cynically seize and display that power, sometimes in order to avoid being perceived as powerless.

Secondly, societies have become increasingly aware of the widespread problem of spousal abuse, some of it physical, much of it psychological. Finally, there is a problem of elder abuse, where elders can be mistreated in rest homes or even when under the care of relatives. We will take a look at each of these areas of potential abuse.

Protecting and Educating Children

Hundreds of books have been published in recent years on bullying among young people. Even though these books mostly talk about bullying in schools, they make some points relevant to our study. When students were asked why they think some students engage in bullying, their answers included "to feel superior and to make victims feel inferior, to be 'cool' or popular, . . . to seek attention. . . . [T]o manipulate the victim, to just have fun, and to get revenge."[1] A very disturbing finding of recent research is that young people who observe others being bullied tend to become hardened to, and indifferent toward, the bullying they witness as they grow older. Fifth graders experience more fear and concern than do eighth graders about the bullying they witness.[2] It's no wonder some authors can say that bullying *teaches* students a "hidden curriculum of peer aggression, power and control," and warn that "in the absence of a whole-school bullying prevention program, the anger and distress expressed by the fifth graders may become the indifference reported by the eighth graders."[3] The "observer" children learn "to develop avoidance skills."[4] Have the majority of the older youth in our churches already learned the "skill" of avoidance and indifference, while a minority engages in bullying and another minority suffers it?

But is there really bullying in youth groups in churches? Many people testify that this is the case. One online writer says "spreading rumors, attacking someone verbally, and intentionally excluding someone from a group are acts of bullying commonly found in our youth groups," and calls us to ask ourselves, "Have we name called, ridiculed, slandered, or personally attacked another?"[5]

Victoria Dinatale is a writer and lecturer who was bullied as a child, and now tries to educate children and adults about and against bullying. She interviewed people whose children had been ostracized at church for asking too many questions. Dinatale says "if you are teaching your children to exclude others, you are teaching them to bully"; in fact, she argues, "Bullying in church happens every time you form a clique and do not include others who are different or less popular."[6] Dinatale recommends introducing oneself to someone new (either new to the church or new to oneself)

1. Espelage and Asidao, "Conversations with Middle School Students," 54.
2. Jeffrey, Miller, and Linn, "Middle School Bullying," 150, 152.
3. Ibid., 153.
4. Ibid.
5. Yates, "Is the Bully Epidemic in Our Churches?"
6. Dinatale, "Bullying Breakdown."

every week, and showing kindness to those who may dress or look differently than oneself.

The element of "looking different" is very important, to adults as well as to young people. We often make our initial judgments about people based on their dress and appearance. It is good practice to try to set aside our tendency to judge, and learn to get to know people. One good piece of advice is this: "Talking about 'different' as interesting, rather than as something to be feared, is critical to growing healthy, accepting children."[7]

I would restate this by saying that we should educate ourselves in *being hospitable*, and then we can educate our children in that same principle. If we adults do not practice hospitality, however, there is no point in trying to force it upon our children. One extremely distasteful adult behavior is the bossy and judgmental way that some parents berate their children in front of others, saying things like "Aren't you going to say hello?" or "What's the matter with you? Why don't you be sociable?" Other adults can help to lubricate such situations by showing graciousness toward all, even toward the boorish parents who are berating their children. I have seen some people who are very skilled at this art of social grace. I myself can sometimes do it, but at other times I become angry and silent, suppressing my urge to yell at the parents, "Why don't you stop bossing and pushing your children around?" I admit that I am sickened by the way many parents belittle their children in public. I will sometimes pick up on something the parent said but leave out the negativity, and communicate that directly to the child. For instance, if a parent said his son was pretty bad at baseball, I might ask the boy, "What position do you like to play?" If a mother said "Suzie is very messy," I might tell Suzie that she has a pretty hat. These techniques do not always yield results, but they sometimes succeed in communicating some degree of respect to the child, and that can be helpful in the long run.

Unfortunately, some children enter society already handicapped. It is an unfortunate feature of child psychology that a child who is bullied by his or her parents will tend to internalize a false

7. Garbarino and deLara, *And Words Can Hurt Forever*, 62.

message, and to take the blame: "Children cannot understand why they should have injuries inflicted on them by the people they love and admire. They therefore reinterpret that behavior and believe it to be right. Cruelty is thus given a positive valuation in the child's cognitive system."[8] Such a child will experience patterns of self-victimization throughout life unless he or she gains psychological insight, learns how to avoid bad patterns of thinking, and manages to develop a network of reliable friends. When one is victimized from an early age, one internalizes false beliefs and learns bad mental habits. It may take a lifetime to unlearn these things.

Unfortunately, verbal abuse and attacks on a child's self-esteem are usually not taken seriously by police or school authorities. Pastors and teachers are "mandated reporters"—obligated to report evidence of physical abuse—but usually there needs to be physical bruising or broken bones before the authorities will take seriously a complaint of abuse. What about evidence of put-downs, name-calling, and the cold and prolonged "soul murder"[9] that some parents commit against their children?[10] When will we become more sensitive to this terrible cruelty? When will we take more seriously Jesus' warning to "not despise one of these little ones," nor to "put a stumbling block before one of these little ones who believe in me. . . . It would be better for you if a great millstone were fastened around your neck and you were drowned in the depth of the sea" (Matt 18:10, 6). Has society ever taken this seriously? Instead, people seem to assume that parents can do anything they want to "their little ones." It would be more Jesus-like to not consider them *their* little ones—their property—at all, but as belonging to God, "for, I tell you, in heaven their angels continually see the face of my Father in heaven" (Matt 18:10). In fact, even adults must "change and become like children" to "enter

8. Miller, *Paths of Life*, 153.

9. The phrase comes from Shengold, *Soul Murder*.

10. Scott Peck tells of his interviews with a set of parents who were coldly dismissive and heartless to their son (*People of the Lie*, 86–108), even giving him his brother's suicide weapon as a Christmas present! (86, 104). Peck rightly examines these parents as an example of evil, but there were no wounds, no signs of beating.

the kingdom of heaven. Whoever becomes humble like this child is the greatest in the kingdom of heaven" (Matt 18:3–4). I do not think Jesus is recommending that adults revert to a child's stage of development; he is highlighting the qualities of interested attention and spiritual receptivity; *those* are what enable anyone (young or old) to grow spiritually. "It is to such as these that the kingdom of God belongs" (Luke 18:16).

Once we have this principle in mind, we need to return to the practical matter of *how* to implement our values.

Peer Supports

A great many books have been published on trying to create a nonbullying culture in the schools. One expert says "What bullies typically need is more structure with very clear expectations about how they should manage their behavior, and what victims need is more peer support. . . . a community of support around each person."[11] Morrison has observed that, "In the majority of cases, the bullying stops within ten seconds when peers intervene."[12] Another expert recommends getting children who are bullied to form a group along with a well-liked counselor and some "good-hearted" fellow students, "not popular kids, but altruistic kids"; this will help young people build social skills and friendships.[13]

Some educators now regularly refer to building up SEL skills (social and emotional learning), which help young people to cope with or defuse bullying. The skills that SEL programs endeavor to impart in schools include 1) learning to notice, identify, and manage one's emotions; 2) developing empathy, including the ability to listen to and think about others' feelings; 3) cooperative problem solving, which often means finding win-win solutions; 4) assertiveness; students are asked to distinguish assertiveness from

---

11. Brenda Morrison, director of the Centre for Restorative Justice, quoted in Goldman, *Bullied*, 233, 235.

12. Ibid., 253.

13. Michael Thompson, in Goldman, *Bullied*, 224.

aggressiveness; 5) building friendships, getting young people to list what behaviors they consider to be friendly.[14]

None of these are simply automatic; teachers and administrators need to be patient and persistent. Students who lack empathy do not suddenly become compassionate because a poster has been put up, but persistent attention to the need to develop empathy and detailed discussion about how bullying affects people will eventually raise the consciousness of children (and adults, for that matter).[15] Students can be asked to role-play to illustrate the difference between attentive listening and distracted "hearing."[16] Students are good at thinking up examples. Role-playing can also be used to illustrate the differing responses to bullying. One student may play the role of bully, insulting someone's dress, while other students are asked to demonstrate a passive response ("yeah, but I love what *you* wear"), an aggressive response ("I got it out of your closet, bitch"), and an assertive response ("Knock it off, Abby").The assertive response signals that the person "does not intend to be victimized," but without name-calling or hostility; it can be spoken unemotionally.[17] Some of these same practices can be implemented in a church youth group if the pastor suspects that disrespect, exclusion, or bullying are happening in the group.

Proceeding on a concept of collaboration, some teachers worked on an activity to teach young people to find diversity interesting.[18] Without separating people into bullies and victims, or even focusing on that problem, teachers may ask the young people to write down and then talk about what "teamwork" means to them, to spell out what behaviors they engage in that they would like to stop, and to write about the effects of bullying upon others.[19] Exercises like this can bring out empathy. Some bullies were or are

---

14. Whitson, *Eight Keys to End Bullying*, 101–15.

15. Ibid., 104–5.

16. Ibid., 106–7.

17. Ibid., 109.

18. Beaudoin and Taylor, *Responding to the Culture of Bullying*, 126–29.

19. Ibid., 160.

themselves bullied, and may have some empathy within them that they have not been encouraged to express.

Recognizing Spousal or Partner Abuse

Verbal abuse, cruelty, and insensitivity must be taken seriously. These are abusive and destructive behaviors. A book written in the 1990s designed to help people recognize abuse in their intimate relationships spoke of some warning signs that there is abuse in intimate relationships: "A whirlwind beginning . . . possessiveness . . . blame . . . verbal abuse . . . insensitivity . . . violence."[20] But it is still abuse if there is only verbal abuse and personal put-downs, and no physical violence. Purely psychological and verbal bullying can be very harmful. And the behavior of the abuser is hardly any different from what we have seen from other kinds of bullies: "Abusers do not take responsibility for the impact of their emotional reactions on others. [They] feel righteous about their anger. . . . The only feelings that matter, are theirs."[21]

Another useful book from the 1990s studies the profiles of batterers and finds that they overwhelmingly fit into the category of borderline personalities. Borderlines are characterized by a weak sense of self, despondency, abandonment anxiety, unawareness of the source of their anger and anxiety,[22] and show "no evidence of learning from mistakes."[23] A borderline personality might actually confuse himself with another person.[24] "Borderline Personality Disorder has several conspicuous similarities to narcissistic personality disorder, but BPD is characterized by self-injury and threatened" suicide.[25] Usually, borderline personalities were

20. Nelson, *Dangerous Relationships*, xi–xvi.

21. Ibid., 137.

22. Dutton, *The Batterer*, 143–48.

23. Ibid., 144.

24. Ibid., 150.

25. American Psychiatric Association, *Diagnostic and Statistical Manual of Mental Disorders IV*, from http://www.halcyon.com/jmashmun/npd/dsm-iv.html.

shamed and humiliated in their youth, and feel a need to shame others.[26] They have a reservoir of fear, shame, and feelings of being rejected, and they deal with them by shaming and rejecting their partners or spouses. In particular, anger is utilized as an "acceptable" emotion for men, but is really being used to cover up fear and shame.[27] Some men, in particular, have an inability to grieve, or to express vulnerability; "despite the male trappings of power, they experience profound powerlessness."[28]

Most of our denominations have literature and sometimes even counselors to help pastors and congregations recognize and deal with spousal abuse. Hopefully the time is permanently behind us where a pastor would counsel a violence victim to stay with the abuser. We have some Bible quotes we can use to help an overly forgiving parishioner to see that leaving is all right: "leave that house" (Matt 10:14). "Do not throw your pearls before swine, or they will trample them under foot" (Matt 7:6). One person who was being abused asked if she should continue forgiving; I said, "No, I don't think so; you have already forgiven him seventy times seven (Matt 18:22), and he only shows contempt. He can't be reached by forgiveness." We need to recognize that there *are* some habitual evildoers who cannot be reached by kindness.

Fortunately, most cities have women's shelters or at least women's centers with counselors and potential allies for the person who is suffering. Every church should keep a list of such resources on hand, possibly posted on a wall or included in the Sunday bulletin.

Protecting Elders

It has increasingly come to the public's attention that many nursing homes are stifling and miserable environments, and that some of the staff are abusive to the elders in their care. We need to be

---

26. Dutton, *The Batterer*, 35.

27. Ibid., 127.

28. Ibid., 179.

skilled observers of our older church members and family members, and learn to pick up on signs of abuse. This can be difficult since many older folks are in various phases of dementia, depression, surliness, and paranoia. We need to increase our psychological awareness, but not use it block out the possibility that some of our elders are not being treated well. Even in a good institution, one or two individual caretakers may be inflicting physical abuse, slapping or otherwise hurting the folks in their care. Caretakers are abusive when they make threats, insult or demean the elderly person, or ridicule him or her for physical limitations. Neglect of the physical health or cleanliness of the patient is also abusive.

The institution, of course, is responsible for monitoring the condition of patients and the way they are treated by the institution's staff. But a pastor who observes signs of abuse or neglect has a responsibility to say something to the institution. Failing a positive response and a change in the quality of care provided, one can report the situation to the Adult Protective Services agency in one's state or municipality.

Abuse can take place in the home, not only in rest homes, and it can even come from a spouse or a son or daughter. It is best to not make assumptions about who "could" or "could not" be an abuser or a target of abuse, but simply to keep our eyes open and think about what we see and hear. It may be necessary for a pastor to discuss suspicions with someone close to the family, someone mature enough to not assume that a troubling question is maliciously motivated. Obviously, we need to be sensitive and professional, not creating new problems unnecessarily, but we also need to be interested in discovering the facts, however unpleasant.

7 - A Way Forward for the Churches

THERE IS NO MAGIC pill that would create an ethical and considerate atmosphere in our churches—just the usual principles of wisdom, respect, and truth. Jesus gave us all the basics. He wanted us to be loving and forgiving, but not to the point of foolishness. If we are forgiving but not wise about the disease of narcissism then we are not being "wise as serpents"; if we only take care of ourselves and are not loving and forgiving, then we are not being "harmless as doves" (Matt 10:16). Here Jesus gives us the principle of balance between kindness and wisdom: we need both. Secular society is now combating bullying in the schools, but bullying continues in the churches because we too often let people take advantage of our inclination to forgive. The church should not lag behind the secular workplace or schoolroom in its ethics. We need to have an ethical procedure for the handling bullies. The amazing forgiveness in Jesus' kingdom does not prevent a just procedure for disciplining slanderers and bullies. There *is* justice, there *is* education, there *is* psychological healing in the kingdom of heaven. Can we bring them into our churches as well?

We can if we have spiritual authenticity and psychological and social wisdom. Jesus gives us advice about authenticity: "Salt is good; but if salt has lost its taste, how can its saltiness be restored?" (Luke 14:34). In other words, our spiritual character is good, unless it has lost its spiritual savor. Then, what good is it? "It is fit neither for the soil nor for the manure pile" (14:35). Do our

83

churches have the right flavor? Do we have the *qualities* (spiritual behaviors), not just the quantities (money and attendants), that we need? Jesus praises the widow for her generosity despite her poverty: "she out of her poverty has put in everything she had" (Mark 12:42–44). I think Jesus is really drawing attention to *quality*, not quantity; it is her *wholeheartedness* that he is praising.

Jesus also taught us about priorities, seeking the will of God first and foremost: "Seek first the kingdom of God and his righteousness, and all these things will be given to you as well" (Matt 6:33). We can make the will of God our central prayer around which all other prayers revolve: "Your will be done, on earth as it is in heaven" (Matt 6:10). And he taught that we *can* do the will of God: "Whoever does the will of God is my brother and sister and mother" (Mark 3:35).

Any church leader who wishes to find effective ways to deal with bullying needs to be fully armed. We need to use the insights of psychology and other contemporary fields of study, but also recognize that Jesus alerted us to these problems in the beginning. We need to become aware of the herd mentality that is common in churches—Jesus already compared disciples to sheep: most people are sheeplike. We need to become aware of the insights of psychology into the harmfulness of cruelty in the home, but Jesus already warned us against offending one of the little ones, and invited the little children to come to him. Girard has exposed the widespread scapegoating pattern in religious groups, but Jesus had already warned his followers that they would be persecuted, and had identified the leaven of the Pharisees as hypocrisy. Sociologists show us the patterns of patronage and social climbing, but Jesus already said not to be like the "benefactors" who "lord it over" others (Luke 22:25), that true leaders must be servants (Matt 23:11).

The churches should be able to take a leadership role in fighting bullying. Besides drawing upon the insights of secular society, we have the truths of the Bible to empower us. We can build an ethic of respect because we can affirm that people are "children of the Most High" (Ps 82:6; see also Matt 23:8–9; John 1:12; Gal 3:26;

Hos 1:10).[1] We believe in a "Spirit bearing witness with our spirit that we are children of God" (Rom 8:16).

Regarding ethics in the church, we should affirm what I call the RASP principles: Respect, Accountability, Support, and Procedure—respecting all the children of God, holding everyone (laypeople and clergy) accountable, supporting and helping each other to "take heart," and following established grievance and other justice-related procedures. The dignity of everyone should be affirmed, but everyone is to be held accountable ("R" and "A"). For that to happen justly, however, churches need to follow the proper procedures that they already have ("P"). And, of course, churches are most successful when they have a genuine warmth, and help people to feel they *belong* ("S").

Respect and support build people up, while accountability and procedure assure that ethical guidelines are observed. Respect and support are individual needs; accountability and procedure are group needs that ultimately protect individuals.

The churches need to make a priority of learning more about the ethics of power, sharing, and responsibility. And we need to make a conscious goal out of gaining a deeper understanding of the psychology of bullying. Those Christians who take this problem seriously, and who educate themselves psychologically, will become ethical leaders in society, which is increasingly interested in fostering healthier environments. Churches should be exemplary places where people can debate and work together in peace, and where young and old can interact and thrive, can "have life, and have it abundantly" (John 10:10).

---

1. For a distinction between the *fact* of sonship with God (referring to spiritual potential) and the *truth* of sonship (living as a child of God), see Finlan, *Options on Atonement*, 36.

Bibliography

American Psychiatric Association. *Diagnostic and Statistical Manual of Mental Disorders.* 4th edition. American Psychiatric Association: 1994. Found at http://www.halcyon.com/jmashmun/npd/dsm-iv.html.

Baker, Sharon L. *Razing Hell: Rethinking Everything You've Been Taught about God's Wrath and Judgment.* Louisville: Westminster John Knox, 2010.

Bandy, Thomas G. *Road Runner: The Body in Motion.* Nashville: Abingdon, 2002.

Basingstoke Circuit Meeting. "Memorial to the Methodist Conference of 2013: Positive Working Together in the Methodist Church." Memorial 28. http://www.methodist.org.uk/media/934451/conf-2013-memorials-final-post-conference-0913.pdf.

Beaudoin, Marie-Nathalie, and Maureen Taylor. *Responding to the Culture of Bullying and Disrespect.* 2nd ed. Thousand Oaks, CA: Corwin, 2009.

Crook, Zeba A. *Reconceptualising Conversion: Patronage, Loyalty, and Conversion in the Religions of the Ancient Mediterranean.* BZNW 130. Berlin: de Gruyter, 2004.

deSilva, David A. *Despising Shame: Honor Discourse and Community Maintenance in the Epistle to the Hebrews.* SBLDS 152. Atlanta: Scholars, 1995.

———. *The Letter to the Hebrews in Social Scientific Perspective.* Eugene, OR: Cascade, 2012.

Dinatale, Victoria. "Bullying Breakdown: Bullies in the church pew." On the *Savannahnow.com* website at http://savannahnow.com/accent/2014-06-30/bullying-breakdown-bullies-church-pew#.U7gHZLcU9Mw

Dutton, Donald G., with Susan K. Golant. *The Batterer: A Psychological Profile.* New York: Basic, 1995.

Eidevall, Göran. "The Role of Sacrificial Language in Prophetic Rhetoric." In *Ritual and Metaphor: Sacrifice in the Bible,* edited by Christian A. Eberhart, 49–61. Atlanta: SBL, 2011.

Erikson, Erik H. *Identity: Youth and Crisis.* New York: Norton, 1968.

Espelage, Dorothy L., and Christine S. Asidao. "Conversations with Middle School Students about Bullying and Victimization: Should We Be Concerned?" In *Bullying Behavior: Current Issues, Research, and Interventions*, edited by Robert Geffner, Marti Loring, and Corinna Young, 49–62. New York: Haworth, 2001.

Finlan, Stephen. "Deification in Jesus' Teachings." In *Theōsis: Deification in Christian Theology*, vol. 2, edited by Vladimir Kharlamov, 21–41. Princeton Theological Monograph Series 156. Eugene, OR: Pickwick, 2011.

———. *Options on Atonement in Christian Thought*. A Michael Glazier Book. Collegeville, MN: Liturgical, 2007.

Garbarino, James, and Ellen deLara. *And Words Can Hurt Forever: How to Protect Adolescents from Bullying, Harassment, and Emotional Violence*. New York: The Free Press, 2002.

Girard, René. *I See Satan Fall Like Lightning*. Translated by James G. Williams. Maryknoll, New York: Orbis, 2001.

———. *Things Hidden Since the Foundation of the World*. London: Athlone, 1987.

———. *Violence and the Sacred*. Translated by Patrick Gregory. Baltimore: Johns Hopkins University Press, 1977.

———. "Violence, Difference, Sacrifice: A Conversation with René Girard." Interview by Rebecca Adams. *Religion and Literature* 25.2 (1993) 9–33.

Goldman, Carrie. *Bullied: What Every Parent, Teacher and Kid Needs to Know about Ending the Cycle of Fear*. New York: HarperOne, 2012.

Haugk, Kenneth C. *Antagonists in the Church: How to Identify and Deal with Destructive Conflict*. Minneapolis: Augsburg, 1988.

Hocking, William Ernest. *The Meaning of God in Human Experience: A Philosophic Study of Religion*. New Haven, CT: Yale University Press, 1912.

Hunt, June. *Bullying: Bully No More*. Torrance, CA: Rose, 2014.

Jeffrey, Linda R., DeMond Miller, and Margaret Linn. "Middle School Bullying as a Context for the Development of Passive Observers to the Victimization of Others." In *Bullying Behavior: Current Issues, Research, and Interventions*, edited by Robert Geffner, Marti Loring, and Corinna Young, 143–56. New York: Haworth, 2001.

Killinger, John. *Outgrowing Church: If the Law Led Us to Christ, to What Is Christ Leading Us?* Eugene, OR: Cascade, 2013.

Kohut, Heinz. *The Analysis of the Self: A Systematic Approach to the Psychoanalytic Treatment of Narcissistic Personality Disorders*. Psychoanalytic Study of the Child, Monograph 4. New York: International Universities Press, 1971.

Lampe, Peter. "Paul, Patrons, and Clients." In *Paul in the Greco-Roman World*, edited by J. Paul Sampley, 488–523. Harrisburg, PA: Trinity, 2003.

Lessing, Doris. "Group Minds." In *Prisons We Choose to Live Inside*, 47-62. New York: Harper & Row, 1987.

Maynard, Dennis R. *When Sheep Attack!* Lexington, KY: Booksure, 2010.

McBirnie, William Steuart. *The Search for the Twelve Apostles*. Carol Stream, IL: Tyndale House, 1973.

McGrath, James F. "Bread and Bullying." December 16, 2013 entry on the "Exploring Our Matrix" blog, www.patheos.com/blogs/exploringourmatrix.

Miller, Alice. *For Your Own Good: Hidden Cruelty in Child-Rearing and the Roots of Violence.* Translated by Hildegarde and Hunter Hannum. New York: Farrar, Straus, and Giroux, 1983.

————. *Paths of Life: Seven Scenarios.* Translated by Andrew Jenkins. New York: Vintage, 1998.

————. *The Untouched Key: Tracing Children Trauma in Creativity and Destructiveness.* Translated by Hildegarde and Hunter Hannum. New York: Doubleday, 1990.

Nelson, Noelle. *Dangerous Relationships: How to Identify and Respond to the Seven Warning Signs of a Troubled Relationship.* Cambridge, MA: Da Capo, 1997.

Orpinas, Pamela, and Arthur M. Horne. *Bullying Prevention: Creating a Positive School Climate and Developing Social Competence.* Washington, DC: American Psychological Association, 2006.

Parker, Erik. "Twelve Reasons Why It Is Good to Be a Church Bully." On the site "The Millennial Pastor." http://millennialpastor.net/2014/01/23/12-reasons-why-it-is-good-to-be-a-church-bully/.

Parker, Robert. "Pleasing Thighs: Reciprocity in Greek Religion." In *Reciprocity in Ancient Greece,* edited by Christopher Gill, Norman Postlethwaite, and Richard Seaford, 105–25. Oxford: Oxford University Press, 1998.

Peck, M. Scott. *People of the Lie: The Hope for Healing Human Evil.* New York: Simon & Schuster, 1983.

Randall, Robert L. *Pastor and Parish: The Psychological Core of Ecclesiastical Conflicts.* New York: Human Sciences Press, 1988.

Rediger, G. Lloyd. *Clergy Killers: Guidance for Pastors and Congregations Under Attack.* Louisville: Westminster John Knox, 1997.

Rice, Joshua. *Paul and Patronage: The Dynamics of Power.* Eugene, OR: Pickwick, 2013.

Rigby, Ken. *New Perspectives on Bullying.* London: Jessica Kingsley, 2002.

Shengold, Leonard. *Soul Murder: The Effects of Childhood Abuse and Deprivation.* New York: Ballantine, 1991.

Talbott, Rick F. *Jesus, Paul, and Power: Rhetoric, Ritual, and Metaphor in Ancient Mediterranean Christianity.* Eugene, OR: Cascade, 2010.

Teykl, Terry. *Preyed On or Prayed For.* Rev. ed. Muncie, IN: Prayer Point, 2000.

Thatcher, Adrian. *Theology and Families.* Challenges in Contemporary Theology. Oxford: Blackwell, 2007.

Van Kaam, Adrian. *Religion and Personality.* Garden City, NY: Image, 1968.

Voegelin, Eric. *From Enlightenment to Revolution.* Durham, NC: Duke University Press, 1975.

Whitlark, Jason A. *Enabling Fidelity to God: Perseverance in Hebrews in Light of the Reciprocity Systems of the Ancient Mediterranean World.* Paternoster Biblical Monographs. Milton Keynes, UK: Paternoster, 2008.

Whitson, Signe. *Eight Keys to End Bullying: Strategies for Parents and Schools.* New York: Norton, 2014.

Wink, Walter. *Engaging the Powers: Discernment and Resistance in a World of Domination.* Minneapolis: Fortress, 1992.

Yates, Karen. "Is the Bully Epidemic in Our Churches?" http://qideas.org/ articles/is-the-bully-epidemic-in-our-churches/

Yoder, John Howard. *The Politics of Jesus: Vicit Agnus Noster.* Grand Rapids: Eerdmans, 1972.

Some Helpful Websites:

Beatbullying.org — aimed largely at youth; has a chat room, news, and links such as "I need to talk" or "I need support from a mentor."

CASEL.org — massive website by the Collaborative for Academic, Social, and Emotional Learning, reporting on educators' efforts to foster social and emotional skills.

GLSEN.org — Gay, Lesbian & Straight Education Network. Articles, news, and links to research.

Kidpower.org — offers programs, videos, blogs about protecting young and old from bullying.

Micheleborba.com — videos, blogs, articles on childhood depression, teaching respect to students, character building, etc.

Overcomebullying.org — hosts discussions and personal reports of bullying; addresses health issues; lists support groups.

Standingvictorious.com — Victoria Dinatale's website tells the story of the 22-year-old overcoming the pain of being bullied. One page includes advice for education majors.

Stopbullying.gov — introduces many aspects of bullying in schools, including how to respond to the problem. Students can watch videos such as "Be More Than a Bystander" and "What is Cyberbullying?."

Thebullyproject.com — interesting "feature" stories and videos about preventing bullying in schools. Has a place to "share your story."

Subject Index

Author Index

Scripture Index

Old Testament

6:47	26	3:28	52
8:34	41	5:13	2
10:4–16	59	5:15	3
10:10	85	5:20	3
10:26–27	59	5:20–21	3
11:26	26	5:23	60
11:50	41, 56	6:1	60
11:52	23	6:2	viii, 62
12:47	22–23		
16:2	14	**Ephesians**	
16:2–3	40		
16:33	22	4:2–3	60
18:23	13, 20	6:1–2	53
21:15–17	59	6:5	53

Acts

		Philippians	
1:13	21	1:6	8
2:42	58	2:13	8

Romans

		Colossians	
8:16	85	3:13	8
12:20	33		
15:2	viii, 62	**Philemon**	

1 Corinthians

		8	53
4:9	2	14	53
4:11	2	16	53
4:13	2	19	53
11:22	52	21	53
12:28	58		
15:28	23	**Hebrews**	
		10:32–33	2
		11:36	2

2 Corinthians

4:6	66	**1 Peter**	
12:20	61	2:23	14, 20

Galatians

		1 John	
1:2	66	3:14	2
3:26	84		

Greek Literature

Homer